The 500 Hidden Secrets of VENICE

THE AUTHOR

While Anna Sardi originally hails from the Veneto, she is a Venetian by passion. She studied architecture, which has helped her understand the city she loves so dearly a little better. However, the biggest help in her quest to discover all of Venice's secrets for this book, came from the many people she met during the writing process. She hopes that this guide not only will tell the stories of many different places, but also those of many different people. Which is why some thanks are necessary:

First and foremost, Anna would like to thank her family, and in particular her aunt Lucia, who was her first reader. Thanks also to Luca, who followed her adventure with all his enthusiasm and passion. Thanks to Fausta, who, when she found out about this project, took Anna under her wing to wander around the city. Their many rambles and conversations helped Anna to see Venice through different eyes, and to see how truly magnificent it is. Thanks to Fosca, because she stands for one of the many faces of Venice, namely erudition. Thanks to Alice and Maria, who were inexhaustible sources of information about new places, and partners in crime to go sample *cicchetti*, among others. Anna herself is very grateful for this; her liver perhaps not so much.

Thanks to Massimo, whose eyes are the same soft hue as the lagoon, and to little Oliver, who showed their boat and a precious part of their world. Thanks to Enrico and Domenico especially, who described what the dawn looks like when he goes fishing, and for so many other things. But above all, Anna would really like to thank Allison: without her this guide would have probably been quite different. Her love of Venice and the lagoon, and the fierce way in which she protects them, will never cease to inspire.

VENICE

overview

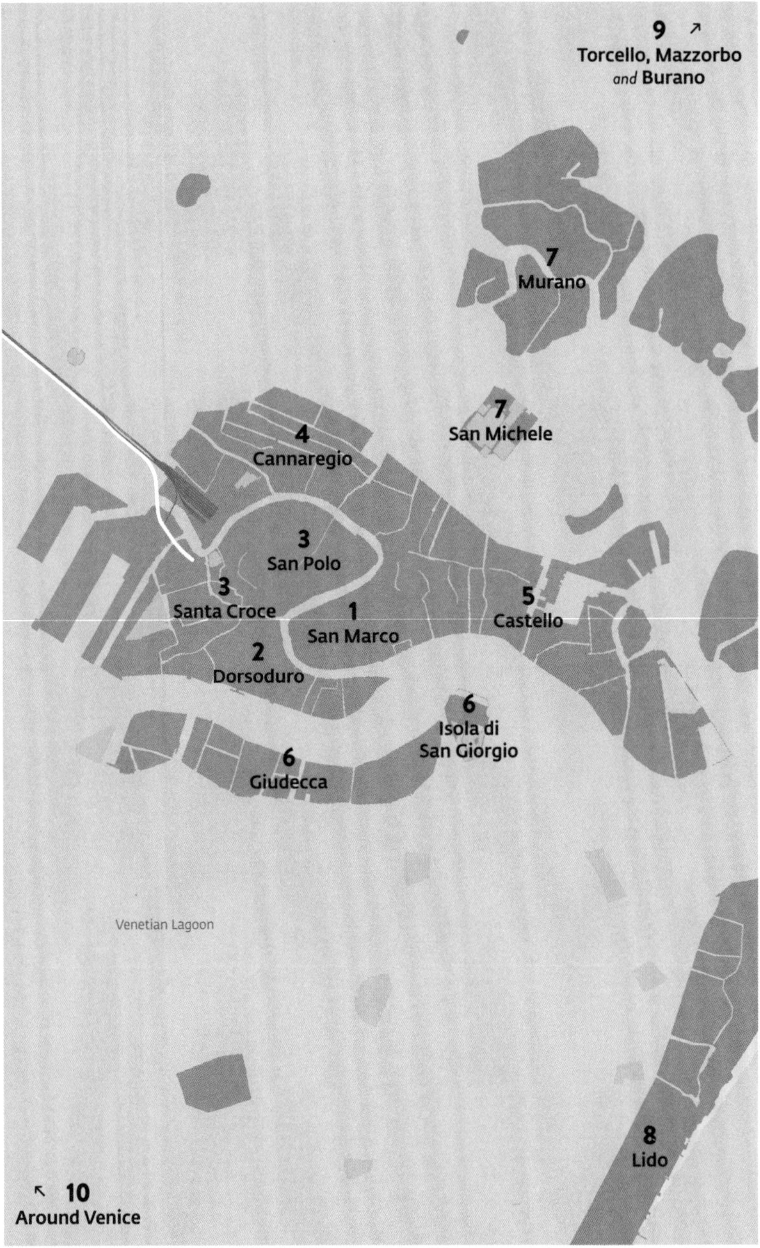
9 ↗
Torcello, Mazzorbo
and Burano
7
Murano
7
San Michele
4
Cannaregio
3
San Polo
3
Santa Croce
1
San Marco
5
Castello
2
Dorsoduro
6
Isola di
San Giorgio
6
Giudecca
Venetian Lagoon
8
Lido
↖ 10
Around Venice

Map 1
SAN MARCO

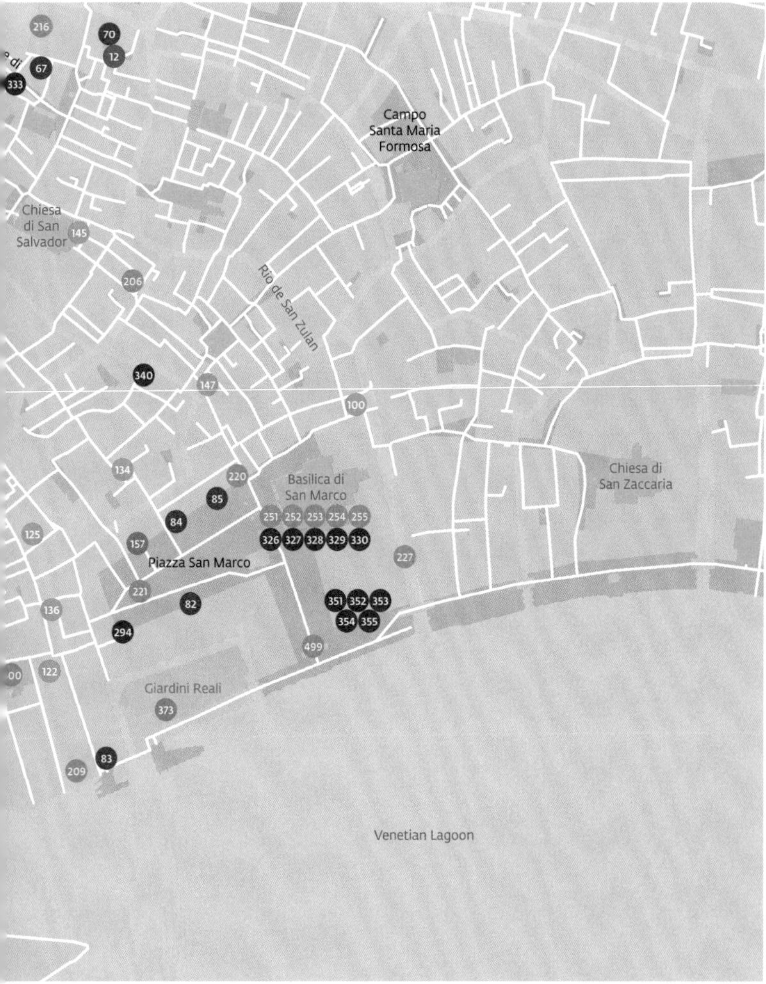
216
70
12
67
333
Campo
Santa Maria
Formosa
Chiesa
di San
Salvador
145
206
Rio de San Zulian
340
147
100
134
220
Basilica di
San Marco
85
84
251 252 253 254 255
326 327 328 329 330
Chiesa di
San Zaccaria
125
157
Piazza San Marco
227
221
82
136
351 352 353
354 355
294
499
122
Giardini Reali
373
83
209
Venetian Lagoon

Map 2

DORSODURO

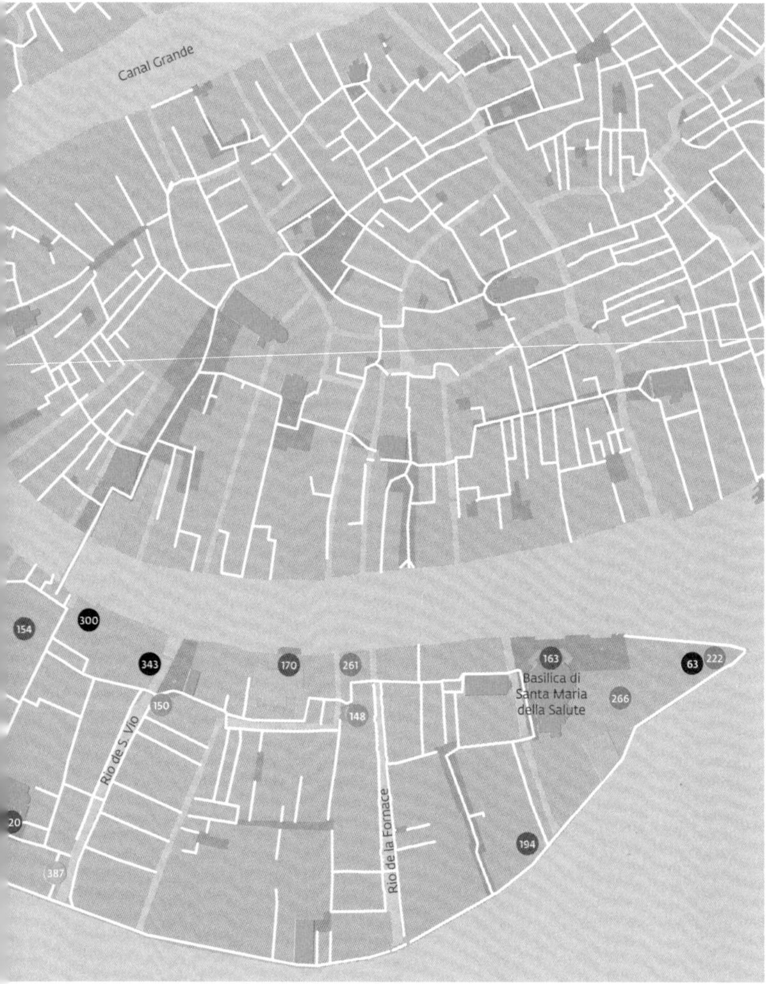
Canal Grande
154
300
343
170
261
163
63
222
150
148
Basilica di
Santa Maria
della Salute
266
Rio de S. Vio
Rio de la Fornace
20
194
387

Map 3
SANTA CROCE *and* SAN POLO

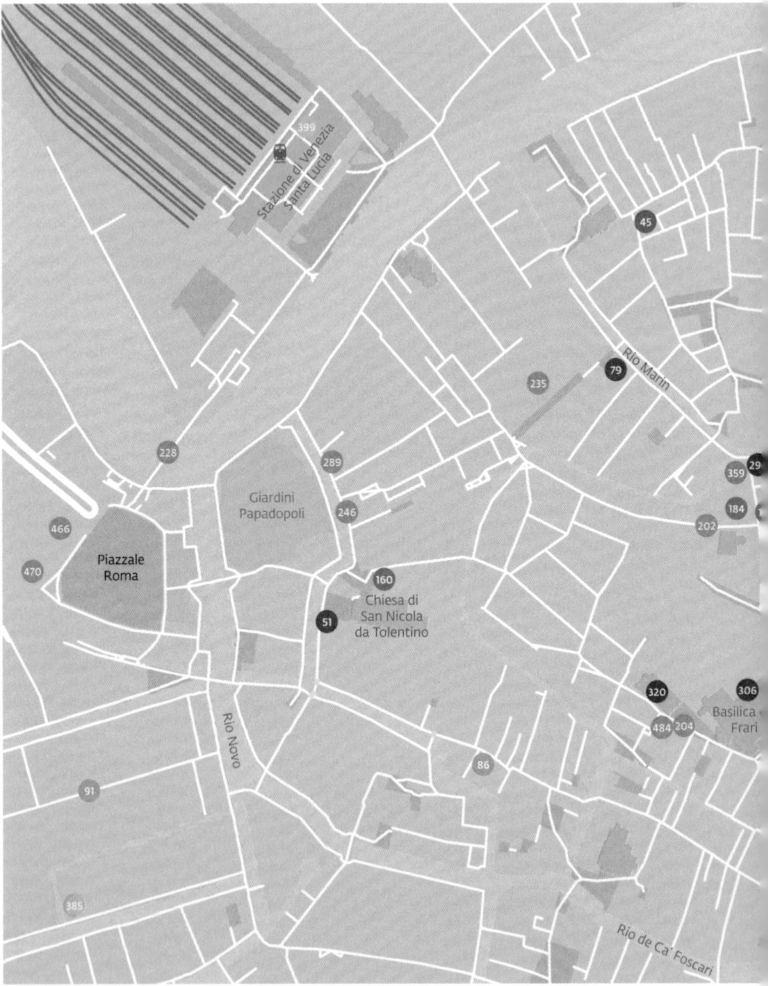

364
Chiesa di
San Stae
64
180
Canal Grande
123
166
344
42
237
203
Rio de lo Do Torre
391
Campo
an Giacomo
dell'Orio
316
88
318
Chiesa di
San Cassiano
230
Campo
della Pescaria
57
369
133
48
471
49
50
309
231
420
47
475
472
15
29
142
130
114
20
112
325
30
333
Ponte di
Rialto
393
482
24
Campo
San Polo
104
68
420
474
Campo di
San Silvestro
44
238
319
106
370
Rio de S. Polo
44
128
Canal Grande

Map 4
CANNAREGIO

Venetian Lagoon
272
Chiesa della
Madonna dell'Orto
263
Rio della Madonna dell'Orto
250
262
496
201
9
9
75
356
342
66
Rio della Sensa
259
224
363
56
182
310
Chiesa dei
Gesuiti
339
10
485
11
205
368
Chiesa di
Santa Fosca
37
Rio di Noale
Rio del Gesuiti
379
Rio Ca' Dolce
213
13
135
287
54
177
Canal Grande
33
38
498
208
Campo
Santi Apostoli
41
211
35
312

Map 5
CASTELLO

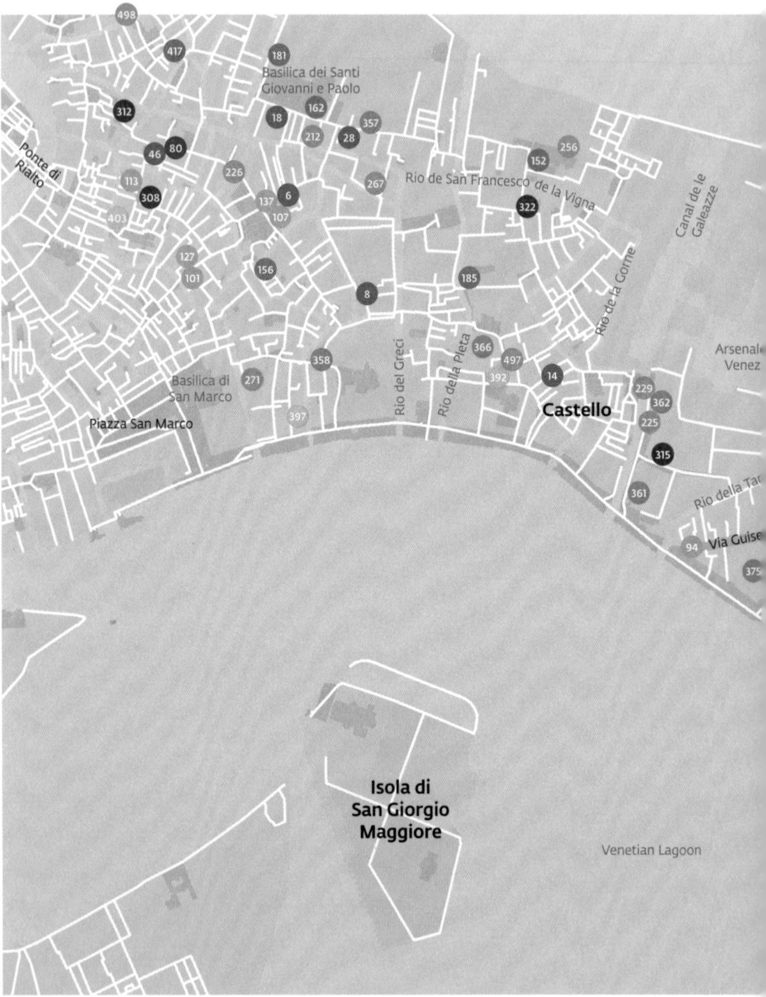

Arsenale di
Venezia
Venetian Lagoon
Giardino delle
Vergini
161
San Pietro
di Castello
338
218
419
64
438
449
La Certosa
81
87
76
158
Rio del Giardini
I Giardini della
Biennale
233
Stadio Pier
Luigi Penzo
Rio de S. Elena
Isola
Sant'Elena
372

Map 6
GIUDECCA *and*

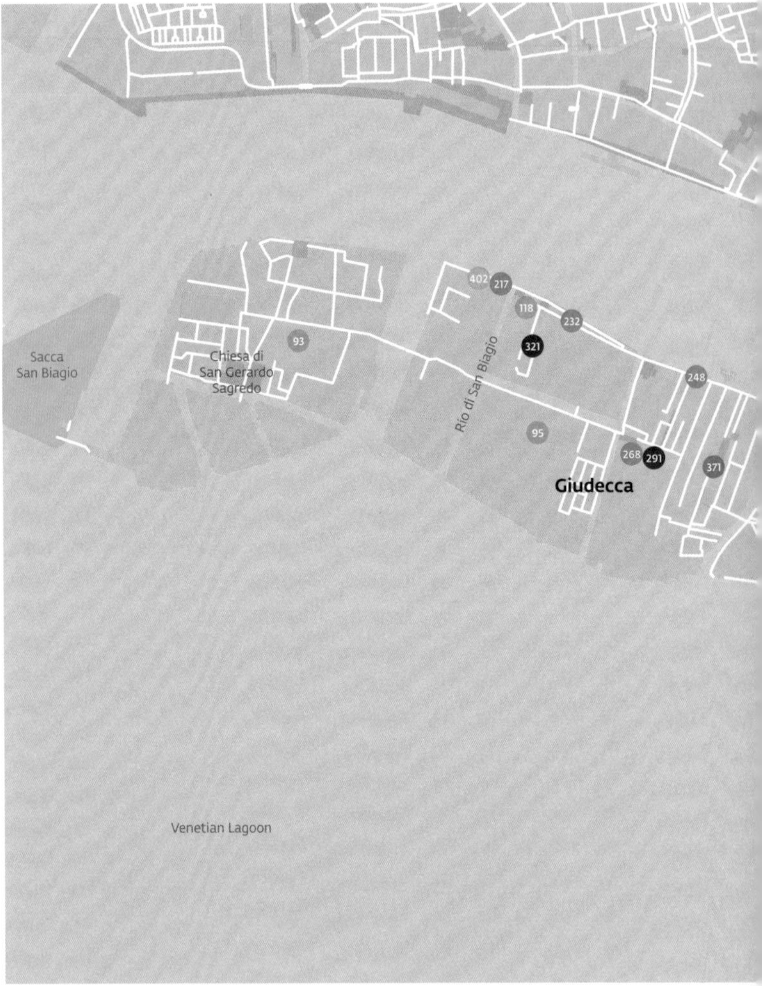

ISOLA DI SAN GIORGIO MAGGIORE

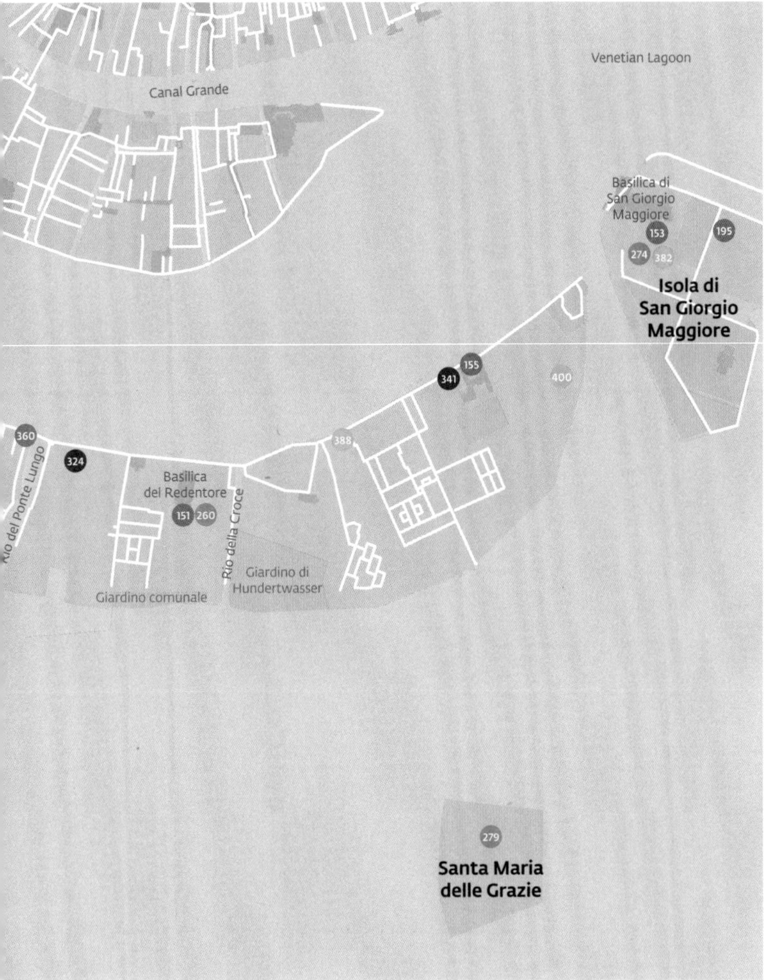

Map 7
MURANO *and* SAN MICHELE

Map 8
LIDO DI VENEZIA *and* ISOLA DELLE ROSE

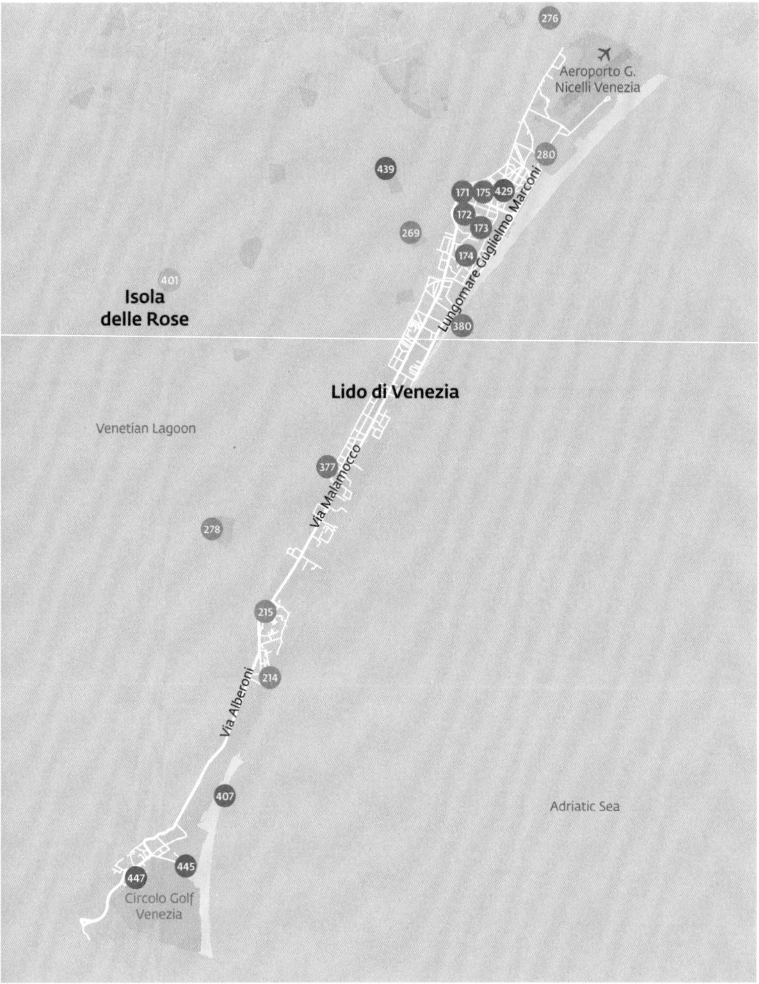

Map 9
TORCELLO, MAZZORBO *and* BURANO

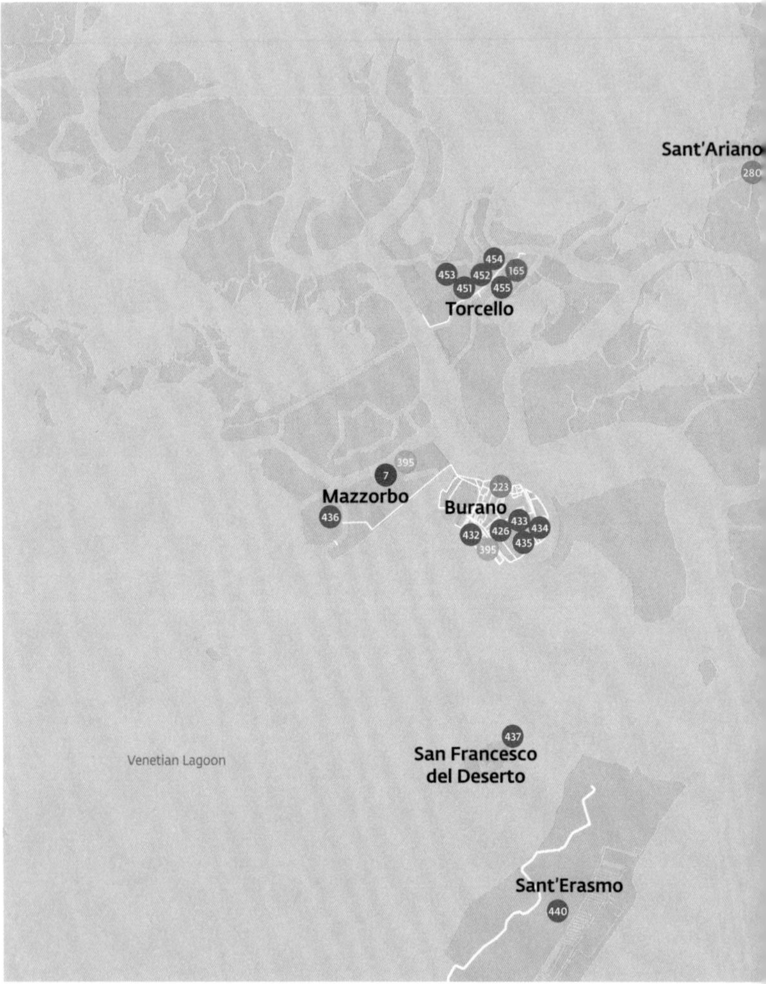

396
Isola Santa Cristina
Venetian Lagoon
Punta Saboni

Map 10
AROUND VENICE

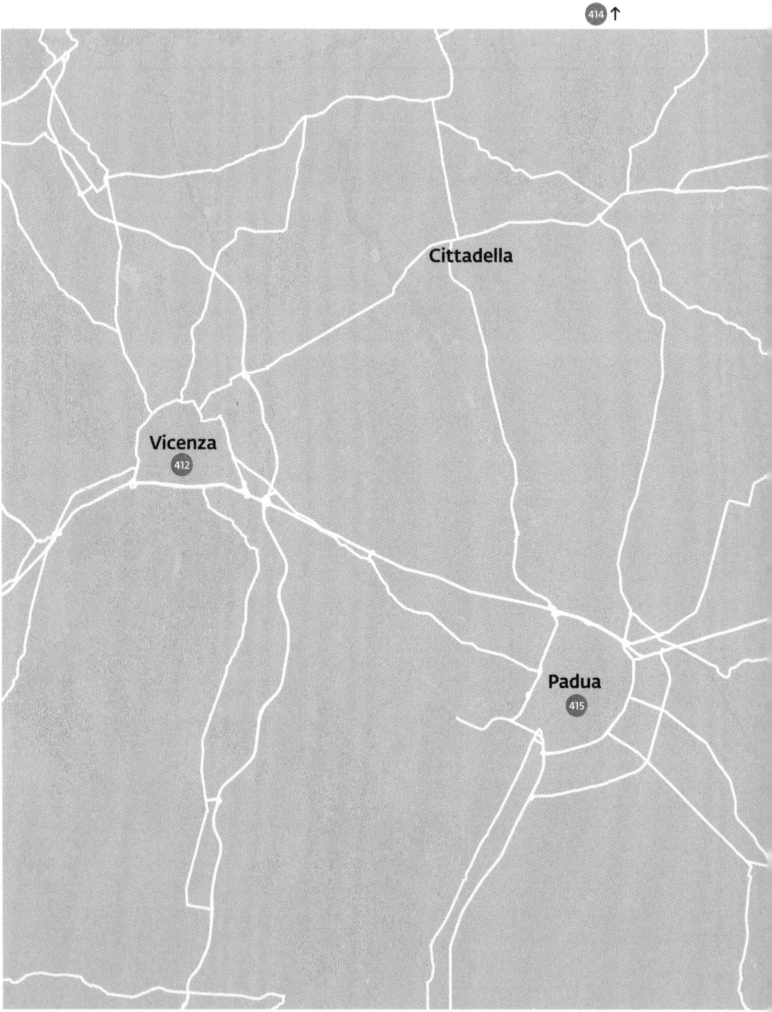

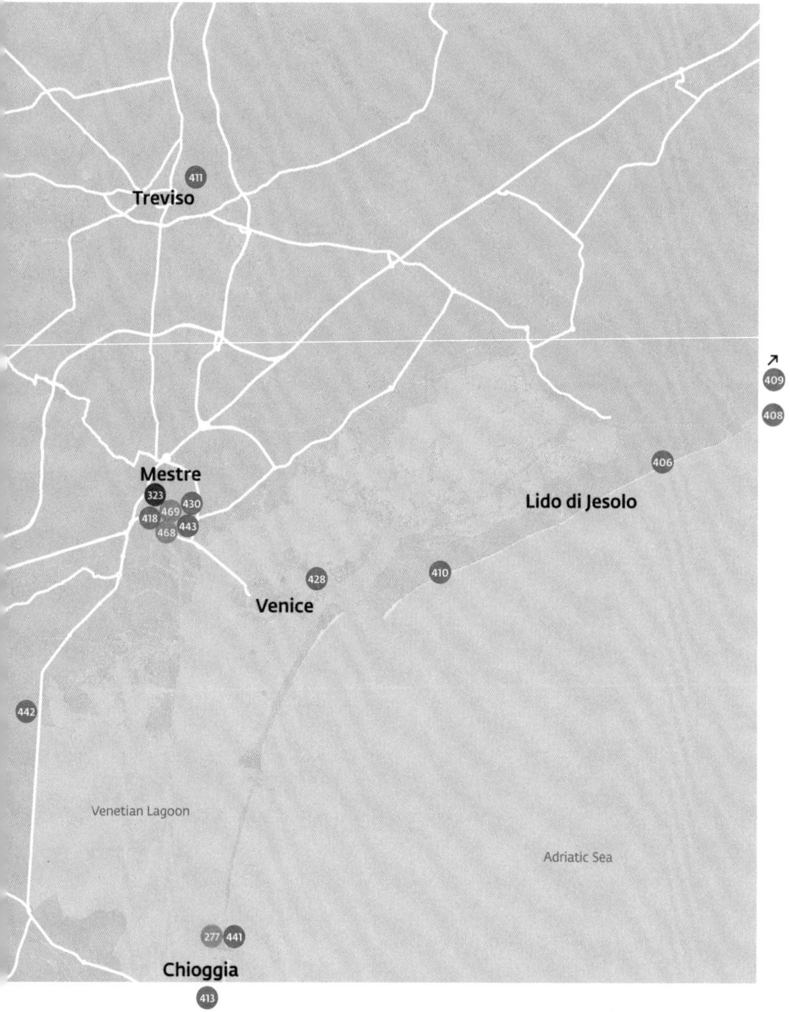
Treviso
411
Mestre
323
430
418
469
468
443
409
408
406
Lido di Jesolo
428
410
Venice
442
Venetian Lagoon
Adriatic Sea
277
441
Chioggia
413

OSTERIA AL MASCARON

USCITA
WINE

50 PLACES TO EAT OR BUY GOOD FOOD

For starters:
5 FOOD & WINE TERMS
you should know

1 **BACARO**

The *bacaro* is the typical Venetian tavern, where, in addition to some excellent lagoon cuisine, you can also score some *ombre* and *cicchetti* – glasses of wine and small snacks to accompany them. Venetians love 'to go for *bacari*' or hop from one tavern to another to enjoy a good glass of house wine together.

2 **OMBRA**

The *ombra* is a half-glass of wine that taverns serve during the *aperitivo* (and beyond). The origin of this term is uncertain but probably refers to the shade under bell towers, which the Venetians sought in the summer, and where they sat down to enjoy a glass of wine.

3 CICCHETTO

Cicchetti are small snacks that are served with the *ombra*. Usually they're eaten before lunch, but now almost all of the taverns and *bacari* serve them all day long. The best are those that reference Venice's local cuisine: creamed stockfish, sardines *in saor* (with onions), polenta and cuttlefish ink.

4 APERITIVO

If you're not a Venetian and you think you know what *aperitivo* is, then think again. First, nobody in Venice will ever call it that and at most they will offer you an *ombra*, or suggest going for *bacari*. This city learned, long before anyone else, that this convivial gathering is a lifestyle. In other words, you still have a lot to learn.

5 SPRITZ

The spritz is the Venetian cocktail *par excellence*. The name derives from the contraction of the German verb *spritzen*, 'to splash', that Austrian troops used when they wanted to water down the wines of the Veneto, which were stronger than what they were accustomed to. Today different variations exist, with Aperol, Campari, Cynar and even Select.

7 VENISSA OSTERIA CONTEMPORANEA

10 RISTORANTE ALGIUBAGIÒ

5 *restaurants that serve excellent*
VENETIAN-STYLE FISH

6 **OSTERIA AL MASCARON**

Calle Lunga Santa Maria Formosa 5225
Castello ⑤
+39 041 522 5995
osteriamascaron.it

A word to the wise: if you decide to eat in this tavern, don't even bother looking at the menu. Find the eccentric owner and ask him for advice. If he likes you, you'll eat the best fish that Venice has to offer (not to mention drink the best wine). This place is not really cheap but it's worth every penny.

7 **VENISSA OSTERIA CONTEMPORANEA**

Fondamenta Santa Caterina 3
Isola di Mazzorbo ⑨
+39 041 527 2281
venissa.it

This tavern has a menu full of amazing dishes for which it sources its ingredients exclusively from the islands in the lagoon. Even the wines are produced in extremely limited quantities and come from the only vineyard on the island of Mazzorbo. An excellent example of traditional cuisine with a contemporary twist and a restaurant that pays special attention to sustainability.

8 LUNA SENTADA

Fondamenta San Severo 5018
Castello ⑤
+39 041 309 7891
lunasentada.it

The philosophy of this wine bar and restaurant is quite intriguing, as it serves traditional Venetian cuisine albeit with a twist. The chef is inspired by Marco Polo's travels, and the many aromas he encountered. Even the plating and the ambience are just slightly different from the typical tavern – just look at the splendid contemporary Murano glass chandelier at the entrance.

9 OSTARIA DA RIOBA

Fondamenta della Misericordia 2553
Cannaregio ④
+39 041 524 4379
darioba.com

Walk by Mr Rioba's statue in the adjacent Campo dei Mori and rub its nose: it will bring you good luck! Although more of a restaurant because of its attitude and menu, this tavern takes its name from the eponymous Venetian legend. The dishes are refined and well presented, the place is pleasant, and has outdoor tables. Excellent fish appetisers.

10 RISTORANTE ALGIUBAGIÒ

Fondamenta Nuove 5039
Cannaregio ④
+39 041 523 6084
algiubagio.net

Whether you stop for a quick breakfast before leaving for the islands, a light lunch, an aperitif overlooking the lagoon, or a fish dinner, this elegant restaurant ticks all the boxes. The menu features traditional dishes, as well as more contemporary options, and even a vegetarian alternative. Something for everyone.

5 places

TOURISTS WILL NEVER EVER FIND

11 **COMBO, VENEZIA**
AT: EX CONVENTO DEI CROCIFERI
Campo dei Gesuiti 4878
Cannaregio ④
+39 041 528 6103
thisiscombo.com

Combo, in the stunning former monastery of the Crociferi order, is a great place to unwind away from the busy, beaten paths of Venice. Stop here for a spritz and some *cicchetti*, in the shade under the orange trees, in the company of students who like to come here to review their notes in the peace and quiet.

12 **BACARANDO IN CORTE DELL'ORSO**
Calle dell'Orso 5495
San Marco ①
+39 041 523 8280

Beware: this *bacaro* is really hard to find, but once you do find it, we know you will not be disappointed. Head for the sofas at the back of the room (if you are lucky enough that it is still unoccupied) and try the house wine with the appetising and abundant *cicchetti*. The salmon and swordfish ones are excellent.

13 **OSTERIA ALLA FRASCA**
Corte de la Carità 5176
Cannaregio ④
+39 041 241 2585

In this homey tavern, you will often find workers and Venetians ordering the specials of the day. During the summer, you can take advantage of the shade and the fresh air in the small backyard, under the boughs (*frasche*). Excellent tuna steak.

14 CORTE SCONTA

Calle del Pestrin 3886
Castello ⑤
+39 041 522 7024
cortescontavenezia.com

Although it's definitely off the beaten track, this tavern is not that difficult to find. However, no one would ever suspect to find such a stunning courtyard, sheltered by lush ivy, behind the entrance facing a narrow alley. The place to go for delicious raw fish.

15 TRATTORIA ANTICHE CARAMPANE

Rio Terà de le Carampane 1911
San Polo ③
+39 041 524 0165
antichecarampane.com

This place is located in the heart of what, during the Most Serene Republic, was the city's red-light district (in Venetian, *carampana* means prostitute). This family-run trattoria serves typical dishes made only with the freshest ingredients, which they source from the nearby Rialto Market, and which are plated with care and contemporary flair.

15 TRATTORIA ANTICHE CARAMPANE

5 bars for an ITALIAN-STYLE BREAKFAST *with a croissant and coffee*

16 **MARCHINI TIME**
Calle de San Luca 4741
San Marco ①
+39 041 241 3087
marchinitime.it

Here breakfast is consumed Venetian-style, meaning standing at the counter, often in a rush and surrounded by the cheerful voices of the waitresses. Order an espresso, a pastry or a croissant, stand in a corner where you won't get in the way of other customers, and observe city life as it flows by.

17 **PASTICCERIA TONOLO**
Calle San Pantalon 3764
Dorsoduro ②
+39 041 523 7209
pasticceria-tonolo-venezia.business.site

Prepare to be amazed as you walk into this bakery and see their long counter of mouth-watering treats. Take your pick from the pastries, cakes, brioches and savoury delicacies. The almond biscuits are particularly delicious.

18 ROSA SALVA

Campo S.S. Giovanni e Paolo 6779
Castello ⑤
+39 041 521 0544
rosasalva.it

The Rosa Salva pastry shop is an institution; since 1879 they have been creating culinary wonders here, thanks to its multiple branches in Venice. Here you'll find sweets of all kinds and a good selection of *tramezzino* sandwiches and savoury snacks. Come early in the morning to take your pick from the great assortment of croissants.

19 PASTICCERIA NOBILE

Calle del Pistor 1818
Cannaregio ④
+39 041 720 731

A historic place and probably one of the best-stocked pastry shops in the centre. The only difficult thing here is choosing, between sweet and savoury, and then between custards, biscuits, cakes, and tiramisu. In any case everything is simply delicious.

20 CAFFÈ DEL DOGE

Calle dei Cinque 609
San Polo ③
+39 041 522 7787
caffedeldoge.com

Just a few steps from the Rialto Bridge you'll find this small cafe, which is renowned for the quality of its coffee blend. Although small, they also have outdoor tables. They also serve soy cappuccinos and vegan croissants here, which are not always easy to find at coffee shops in Venice.

18 **ROSA SALVA**

5 restaurants for
ETHNIC CUISINE

21 ORIENT EXPERIENCE

Rio Terà Farsetti 1847/B
Cannaregio ④
+39 041 822 4337

The history of this restaurant alone is worth a visit. Hamed Ahmadi arrived in Italy in 2006. After being granted refugee status and organising several cultural activities at the reception centre, he opened this place where refugees cook the dishes they've become accustomed to on their travels to Italy. He currently owns five restaurants.

22 AFRICA EXPERIENCE

Calle Lunga San Barnaba 2722
Dorsoduro ②
+39 041 476 7865
africaexperience.eu

Africa Experience is Hamed's second achievement: after the rotisserie and the restaurant that serves refugees' recipes, he opened a restaurant specialising in African dishes, from Egypt, Gambia, Senegal, Nigeria and many other countries. The philosophy is always the same: a menu that refers to travel and food as a means of social awareness.

23 **SUDEST 1401**

Palazzo delle Zattere 1401
Dorsoduro ②
+39 041 099 6843

The latest project by Hamed Ahmadi, and curated by his longtime partner Alì Rezai, again references cultural cross-pollination, but this time with a different geographical area. As the name suggests, the restaurant's cuisine is based on the fusion of Sicilian and Balkan dishes. The menu changes according to the seasons and the inspiration of the cooks.

24 **FRARY'S**

Fondamenta dei Frari 2558
San Polo ③
+39 041 720 050
frarysvenezia.it

This place is just a short walk from the Basilica dei Frari and serves colourful Middle Eastern inspired fare, with a foray into Greek cuisine. The varied menu includes lots of vegetarian, vegan and gluten-free options (the restaurant obtained AIC ITALIA certification for gluten-free food).

25 **IGUANA**

Calle del Aseo 1885
Cannaregio ④
+39 041 476 3749
iguanavenezia.com

In this lively restaurant you can take a break from the ubiquitous spritz and enjoy a piña colada or other colourful cocktail instead. They also serve tortillas, made fresh daily, and generous portions of Mexican dishes, all at reasonable prices.

5 *restaurants for*
GOOD PIZZA
(and more)

26 **IL REFOLO**
Ramo Quinto Gallion O del Pezzetto 1459
Santa Croce ③
+39 041 524 0016

This restaurant gives out onto a tiny intimate square along a canal. The locals like to dine at the outdoor tables in the summer and enjoy the *refolo*, or gentle breeze you always feel here. In the evening, you can enjoy a romantic candle-light dinner under the stars. The menu includes pizza, meat and fish dishes.

27 **ACQUA PAZZA**
Campo Sant'Anzolo 3808
San Marco ①
+39 041 277 0688
veniceacquapazza.com

Finding a good pizza in Venice is definitely not an easy feat. Acqua Pazza serves excellent fish dishes as well as a thick and fragrant pizza with top-quality ingredients. The restaurant is located in a quiet campo with outdoor tables. While the prices are not the cheapest in town, the food here is definitely worth it.

28 **PIZZERIA ALLA STREGA**
Barbaria de le Tole 6418
Castello ⑤
+39 041 528 6397

There are very few real pizzerias in Venice (if you don't consider the take-outs that have popped up everywhere lately). This one has been holding its ground since 1979 and serves excellent calzones, pizzas with an organic crust, and delicious homemade tiramisu.

29 **NOVECENTO JAZZ CLUB 900**

Campiello del Sansoni 900
San Polo ③
+39 041 522 6565

This excellent pizzeria is located in the heart of Venice, on a quiet *campiello*. The crunchy, thin crust of their pizzas and the laidback ambience make this place so special. Wash your pizza down with a glass of beer and a side of jazz, with occasional live performances.

30 **BIRRARIA LA CORTE**

Campo San Polo 2168
San Polo ③
+39 041 275 0570
birrarialacorte.it

Although the pizza at this brewery is excellent and prepared with fresh ingredients and with unexpected toppings, the first courses are equally good. The many varieties of beers on tap are also worth mentioning. The restaurant is located in Campo San Polo, one of the most beautiful in Venice, and has a large front of house and outdoor tables.

5
BACARI
where Venetians love to go

31 **BACHARO TOUR**
bacharotour.com

A brilliant idea by two locals who wanted to take 'cultured' music out of the hallowed halls and bring it to places where you would never expect to hear it, like Venice's *bacari* for example. Every year, in May and June, the association organises travelling concerts, with artists performing while people sit back and enjoy their glass of wine and *cicchetti*. Check their Facebook page for more details.

35 OSTARIA AL PONTE

32 **AL TIMON BRAGOZZO**
Fondamenta dei Ormesini 2754
Cannaregio ④
+39 041 524 6066
altimon.it

Exposed bricks, a counter with a generous spread of *cicchetti*, excellent spritz and *ombre*, a relaxed atmosphere: this typical Venetian tavern ticks all the boxes. There is only one difference: the house speciality is meat and not fish. A must-try!

33 **TRATTORIA DA BEPI GIÀ '54'**
Campo S.S. Apostoli 4550
Cannaregio ④
+39 041 528 5031
dabepi.it

A place where you can experience the real Venice. The interior of this traditional trattoria, with its wood-panelled walls and exposed beams, provides the perfect setting to sample simple, unfussy Venetian cuisine. In autumn and spring, you should definitely try their fried *moeche*, or soft shell crabs. This delicacy is becoming increasingly difficult to find.

34 **CACONERO**
Fondamenta Barbarigo 2344
Dorsoduro ②
+39 041 524 6042
caconero.it

If you need a break from Venetian cuisine and are looking for a more international menu, then head to Caconero. This large bistro – opened in 2017 – off the tourist trail, is popular with university students and for business lunches. Try their varied and tasty salads and their homemade cakes.

35 **OSTARIA AL PONTE**
Calle Larga Giacinto Gallina 6378
Cannaregio ④
+39 041 520 2747

An amazing selection of *cicchetti* and cheeses, a good wine list and reasonably-priced spritzes: in short, this historic restaurant has it all and if you wish to stop for a more substantial meal, the fish dishes are definitely worth trying.

5 trattorias where you should order the
SPECIAL OF THE DAY

36 **TRATTORIA DALLA MARISA**
Fondamenta
San Giobbe 652
Cannaregio ④
+39 041 720 211

One of the few *bacari* where the fixed menu caters to the employees and students of nearby Ca' Foscari University rather than to tourists. The place is small and rather rustic but, weather allowing, you can sit at the tables along the canal.

37 **OSTERIA AL CANTINON**
Sottoportego delle
Colonete 2152
Cannaregio ④
+39 041 524 3801
osterialcantinon.it

In this intimate restaurant, which is more refined than the average tavern, you can enjoy an excellent fish dish at the romantic tables that overlook the canal. Enjoy the peace and quiet even though you are just a few steps from the Strada Nova.

38 **HOSTARIA BACANERA**
Campiello de
la Cason 4506
Cannaregio ④
+39 041 260 1146
bacanera.business.site

This restaurant, which is managed by a group of young Venetians, is synonymous with quality and freshness. There are just a few dishes on their seasonal menu, which changes depending on what's available at the Rialto market. Here they still believe in tradition, smoking, fermenting and dehydrating their ingredients, following their imagination wherever it leads. The result is always something good.

39 OSTERIA DA CODROMA

Fondamenta Briati 2540 Dorsoduro ②
+39 041 524 6789

You'll find this typical tavern along Fondamenta Briati, which is a great place a stroll away from the tourist routes. Order a couple of *cicchetti* or a more abundant meal. In the latter case, it's best to start with the long list of bountiful appetisers.

40 LA PALANCA

Fondamenta Sant'Eufemia 448 Giudecca ⑥
+39 041 528 7719

La Palanca is a must if you decide to visit the island of Giudecca. Sit at one of the tables with the most beautiful view of the Zattere across the canal and enjoy some excellent Venetian fish dishes. If you fancy a snack choose the *tramezzino* sandwiches. In any event, any meal with such a delightful view makes for a truly restorative experience.

5 *excellent* ICE-CREAM *parlours*

41 **DA NICO**
Fondamenta Zattere
Al Ponte Longo 922
Dorsoduro ②
+39 041 522 5293
gelaterianico.com

People have been flocking here for Nico's legendary *gianduiotto* for many years, and it has truly become a Venetian institution as a result! Do try this amazing creation, which is made from a piece of *gianduia* (a mix of chocolate and hazelnuts) served in a small cup and covered with lashings of whipped cream. Exquisite is an understatement.

41 DA NICO

42 GELATO DI NATURA

Campo San Giacomo dell'Orio 1628
Santa Croce ③
+39 340 286 7178
gelatodinatura.com

This ice-cream shop has several franchises in the city. While it doesn't have many flavours and some are on rotation, the quality of the ingredients is excellent, and the ice cream simply delicious. Do try their walnut and fig if it's available.

43 GELATERIA PAOLIN

Campo Santo Stefano 2962
San Marco ①
+39 041 522 5576

You'll find the Paolin ice-cream parlour in Campo Santo Stefano, one of the most beautiful squares in Venice. This large venue has many outdoor tables. The perfect setting – especially on a hot summer's day – for a break and a cup that overflows with fruit and ice cream.

44 GELATERIA IL DOGE VENEZIA

Calle Traghetto Vecchio 2822
San Polo ③
+39 339 148 2164

One of Venice's oldest *gelaterias*, which is very centrally located and the perfect place for a break in between visits to monuments. They serve excellent, strictly artisanal ice cream, including classic and more experimental flavours, with a few dairy and gluten-free options.

45 GELATERIA ALASKA

Calle Larga dei Bari 1159
Santa Croce ③
+39 041 715 211

The artisan *gelato* shop par excellence. This hole in the wall produces only a few flavours, depending on which ingredients are available and in season. The ice cream is less sweet than others, as the ice-cream maker prefers to focus on the depth of flavour. Truly outstanding.

5 *hidden bacari and taverns* NEAR RIALTO

46 **OSTERIA AL PORTEGO**
Calle de la Malvasia Vechia 6014
Castello ⑤
+39 041 522 9038
osteriaalportego.org

Despite being in a strategic (i.e. touristic) location, between San Marco and Rialto, this small *bacaro* remains true to itself and to Venetian cuisine. Here you can find the typical *cicchetti* and a good selection of wines. Do book ahead if you want to eat here.

47 **OSTERIA BANCOGIRO**
Campo San Giacometto 122
San Polo ③
+39 041 523 2061
osteriabancogiro.it

This tavern is located at the foot of the Rialto Bridge and serves absolutely delicious, plentiful and reasonably priced *cicchetti*. Also a good place for a light lunch. If you want something more substantial, order a fish dish, ideally sitting at one of the tables in the back, which overlook the Canal Grande.

48 **CANTINA DO SPADE**
Sotoportego de le do Spade 859
San Polo ③
+39 041 521 0583
cantinadospade.com

As you walk into this *bacaro*, you'll see a beautiful wooden bar with an amazing array of *cicchetti*, a large quantity of wine bottles, and a wood-panelled room with colourful paintings on the walls. Their fried foods are delicious, and can be eaten as *cicchetti* or a main course. The fried fish platter is copious, light, and delicious.

49 CANTINA DO MORI

Calle do Mori 429
San Polo ③
+39 041 522 5401

Cantina do Mori is one of the oldest bars in Venice. Here you'll see copper pots hanging from the ceiling, with demijohns of wine everywhere, and the most extraordinary *cicchetti*, to be enjoyed standing in keeping up with local custom. The prices are slightly above average but the quality makes up for this.

50 ALL'ARCO

Calle Arco 436
San Polo ③
+39 041 520 5666

This little *bacaro* is located in one of the thousand alleys near Rialto. There are no seats, so this is definitely a place for a snack or a quick *aperitivo*, but its bountiful and appetizing *cicchetti* are always worth the stop. The creamed stockfish is excellent.

46 OSTERIA AL PORTEGO

VINO-VERO

35 PLACES TO HAVE A DRINK

5 *places to drink*
ON A BUDGET

51 **BACARETO DA LELE**
Campo dei Tolentini 183
Santa Croce ③
+39 347 846 9728

At any given time of the day, this tiny *bacaro* is always packed with students and Venetians chatting along the *fondamenta* facing the canal. This is largely because of the low prices they charge for *ombre* and *cicchetti*. While they don't have a huge selection of food, it's definitely appetising.

52 **AL CHIOSCHETTO**
Fondamenta Zattere Al Ponte Lungo 1406/A
Dorsoduro ②
+39 348 396 8466

A small and unpretentious bar with a breathtaking view. This kiosk is located on one of the widest and most beautiful promenades in Venice. Around *aperitivo*, it's not uncommon to find groups of friends armed with spritzes, sitting on the ground while watching the sun set over the lagoon.

53 **CHET BAR**
Campo Santa Margherita 3638
Dorsoduro ②
+39 328 419 9252

If you need a break from the omnipresent spritz, this cocktail bar is the perfect place for you. The drinks menu includes the usual suspects as well as a few bolder suggestions. After dinner this is a popular place with university students.

54 **EL SBARLEFO**
Salizada del Pistor 4556/C
Cannaregio ④
+39 041 524 6650
elsbarlefo.it

A tiny *bacaro* with a good selection of *cicchetti*, *ombre* and cocktails. But the menu also features more robust options, including a dinner consisting of raw fish with paired wines. On Fridays and Saturdays they host jazz and blues concerts. Their other *bacaro* is at Dorsoduro 3757.

55 **CANTINE DEL VINO GIÀ SCHIAVI**
Fondamenta Nani 992
Dorsoduro ②
+39 041 523 0034
cantinaschiavi.com

An authentic wine bar, with wooden beams and floor-to-ceiling shelves that are heaving under the weight of the wine bottles. One of the few places in the city where you can still enjoy a glass of white house wine and some delicious *cicchetti* for just a few euros.

51 BACARETO DA LELE

5 bars where you can enjoy
A GREAT SPRITZ

56 **CANTINA VECIA CARBONERA**
Rio Terà della Maddalena 2329
Cannaregio ④
+39 041 710 376

A typical Venetian local, furnished with barrels and demijohns. The variety of wines and snacks is vast, and the spritz, which is also available 'to go', is excellent. If you're lucky, you may find a spot at the table with a romantic view of the canal.

60 OSTERIA AL SQUERO

57 **OSTERIA DA FILO**
Rio Terà Primo 1539
Santa Croce ③
+39 041 524 6554

An informal and welcoming space, with leather sofas, origami and paper lanterns. During the day, head to Da Filo for a drink in a laidback, cosy spot. In the evenings, the place is packed with young people and definitely becomes livelier. On Wednesdays they always host live music performances.

58 **OFICINA ORMESINI**
Fondamenta degli Ormesini 2689
Cannaregio ④
+39 348 341 5910
oficinaormesini.com

You have two options here: sit down at one of the tables and enjoy some people watching while you sip your (excellent) spritz. Alternatively, you can start your evening with an *aperitivo*, followed by some delicious *cicchetti*, superb fish starters, a nice mix of meat or fish for your main and a *digestivo* to top it all off.

59 **AL PARLAMENTO**
Fondamenta Savorgnan 511
Cannaregio ④
+39 041 244 0214
alparlamento.it

This beautiful place is off the beaten track of most of the tourist itineraries and is a real institution for university students, and beyond. Here you can get anything from abundant *cicchetti* and *tramezzino* sandwiches to spritz and other classic cocktails.

60 **OSTERIA AL SQUERO**
Fondamenta Nani 943-944
Dorsoduro ②
+39 335 600 7513
osteriaalsquero.wordpress.com

No matter what time of day or night you decide to stop at this little *bacaro*, it is always packed with tourists and Venetians alike. That's because the *cicchetti* and spritz are excellent, but, above all, because you can take your plate and glasses outside and enjoy your aperitif with a view of the canal and the gondola shipyard on the other side. Particularly nice during the summer.

5 *wonderful* MUSEUMS *where you can enjoy* A CUP OF TEA

61 **OMBRA DEL LEONE**
Calle del Ridotto 1364
San Marco ①
+39 041 241 3519
ombradelleone.com

The highlight of this restaurant (nestled inside Ca' Giustinian) is, without a doubt, the splendid terrace with a panoramic view of the Church of Santa Maria della Salute and the lagoon. Stop here for a tea, an aperitif or dinner: at any time of the day the atmosphere is simply enchanting.

62 **PALAZZO GRASSI CAFÉ**
AT: PALAZZO GRASSI
Campo San Samuele 3231
San Marco ①
+39 041 240 1308
palazzograssi.it

Palazzo Grassi's bistro cafe is a bright, minimal space overlooking the Canal Grande. The ideal place to quietly sip a cup of tea and watch the crowds pass by under the large windowsill. They also have some excellent lunch options if your hunger pangs interfere with your contemplation.

63 **DOGANA CAFÉ**
AT: MUSEO DI PUNTA DELLA DOGANA
Fondamenta Salute 2
Dorsoduro ②
+39 041 240 1308
palazzograssi.it

The Punta della Dogana museum is perhaps one of the most beautiful museums in Venice. What better way to wrap up your visit with a nice cup of hot tea or perhaps a gourmet aperitif? The cafeteria and the bookshop are in the same room, an excellent opportunity to enjoy an interesting read during your break.

64 **CAFFETTERIA DI CA' PESARO**

Fondamenta de Ca' Pesaro 2076
Santa Croce ③
+39 041 721 127
capesaro.visitmuve.it

The cafe at Ca' Pesaro is quite small, but if you are lucky enough to secure one of the few tables available, you can enjoy some tea and a lovely selection of pastries just a few steps from the Canal Grande.

65 **CAFFETTERIA DI CA' REZZONICO**

Fondamenta Rezzonico 3136
Dorsoduro ②
+39 041 241 0100
carezzonico.visitmuve.it

This beautiful museum, which is dedicated to the 18th century in Venice, has a garden as well as a cafe in the hallway, with a fine selection of coffee blends, where weary visitors can rest their feet. The view on the Canal Grande is included for free.

62 **PALAZZO GRASSI CAFÉ**

5 *quality*
WINE BARS

66 **VINO-VERO**
Fondamenta de la Misericordia 2497
Cannaregio ④
+39 041 275 0044

Beware: you won't find any spritz or cocktails in this tiny wine bar. They do have an excellent selection of wines by the glass and the bottle. Perhaps the latter are a bit more expensive than average, but they are worth every penny. The *cicchetti* are fancy and absolutely delicious. So is the atmosphere of the place: soft jazz, friendly staff and outdoor tables.

67 **MILLEVINI**
Ramo del Fontego dei Tedeschi 5362
San Marco ①
+39 041 520 6090

A small but well-stocked wine shop right behind Fondaco dei Tedeschi. Millevini has wines for every palate and pocket, with prices ranging from low to high. The selection of liqueurs is also excellent and sophisticated. Some excellent gift ideas to be found here, too.

68 **VINERIA ALL'AMARONE**
Calle Sbianchesini 1131
San Polo ③
+39 041 523 1184
allamarone.com

The name of this wine bar refers to one of the top wines in the the Veneto region (Amarone) and definitely lives up to its name. In a room lined from top to bottom with bottles, you can taste typical dishes, *cicchetti*, and first courses of fish, each paired with the most appropriate wine.

69 **ENOTECA AL VOLTO**
Calle Cavalli 4081
San Marco ①
+39 041 522 8945
enotecaalvolto.com

The Enoteca Al Volto is a historic place in Venice, which opened its doors in 1936. You'll immediately appreciate the friendly atmosphere and the unpretentious, simple look of the room with exposed beams as you walk in. The menu features earthy *ombre* and *cicchetti*, and excellent specials of the day.

70 **I RUSTEGHI**
Corte del Tentor 5513
San Marco ①
+39 338 760 6034
airusteghi.com

In Venice's most touristic and crowded areas, you'll stumble upon a tiny, secluded courtyard, and this beautiful wine bar. The food options are not limited to *cicchetti*, but also include delicious platters of cheese and cold cuts.

5 places for
A LATE NIGHT DRINK

71 **B BAR LOUNGE**
AT: BAUER HOTEL
Salita San Moise 1459
San Marco ①
+39 041 520 7023
bauervenezia.com

The elegant lounge bar of the decidedly luxurious Hotel Bauer is a good alternative if you're fed up with the ubiquitous spritz and need something stronger. This place, with its muted light and soft leather armchairs, is a real treat on cold winter evenings. It's open late and often hosts jazz and blues concerts.

72 **OSTERIA ALLA BIFORA**
Rio Terà de la Scoazzera 2930
Dorsoduro ②
+39 041 523 6119

This typical osteria, which serves authentic family food, is open quite late. Do taste their copious and appetising platters of cheese and cold cuts, and don't forget to order a nice glass of Prosecco with it!

73 **TARNOWSKA'S AMERICAN BAR**
Campo Santa Maria del Giglio 2494
San Marco ①
+39 041 520 8333

While not necessarily cheap, this elegant 1950s-inspired bar serves excellent cocktails, mixed with only the best ingredients. Pro tip: as you sip your drink, find out more about the intriguing story of the woman after whom the bar was named.

74 BAKARÒ DO DRAGHI

Calle de la Chiesa 3665
Dorsoduro ②
+39 041 241 2758
bakaro.it

A welcoming place, with an urban look and feel, that serves cocktails, beer and has an international menu, next to the usual spritz and *cicchetti*. The atmosphere heats up in the evening, when even Campo Santa Margherita is filled with young people. Although it's quite roomy, you'll often find groups of friends sipping a beer outside on the street.

75 PARADISO PERDUTO

Fondamenta della Misericordia 2540
Cannaregio ④
+39 041 720 581
ilparadisoperduto.wordpress.com

As you walk into this tavern, it is really difficult not to be mesmerised by the imposing bar, which is loaded with all kinds of delicacies. The bad news is that, as this place is very popular, it's often too crowded and they don't take reservations. The good news is that it's open a little longer than the other *bacari*, so you'll have more time to enjoy the food.

75 PARADISO PERDUTO

5 places for an excellent ESPRESSO

76 **CAFFÈ ROSSO**
Campo Santa Margherita 2963
Dorsoduro ②
+39 041 528 7998
cafferosso.it

A historic bar in Venice, which was founded by a fisherman at the end of the 19th century. In the early 20th century, its walls witnessed many a heated political discussion, as well as plenty of tricks played on the patrons of another bar in Campo Santa Margherita. Today the bar's oldest employee is its espresso machine.

77 **BAR AI ARTISTI**
Calle Lunga San Barnaba 2771
Dorsoduro ②
+39 346 960 7785

This small bar overlooks the elegant Campo San Barnaba and comes with a beautiful view of the church of the same name – a good place for a stop 'with a view'. To be fair, they don't serve much else besides coffee and wine but they are both excellent, which makes up for the short menu.

76 **CAFFÈ ROSSO**

78 **OSTARIA AL PONTE**

Calle Seconda de la Fava 930 Castello ⑤
+39 339 831 2584

Excellent coffee and much more. The walls of this classic tavern, which is perched on the steps of the bridge leading towards Fondamenta Dandolo, are painted red, adding to the warm and welcoming atmosphere... Often packed with people.

79 **PASTICCERIA RIO MARIN**

Fondamenta Rio Marin 784 Santa Croce ③
+39 041 718 523

This pastry shop with outdoor seating is located just a short walk from the station. The coffee is delicious, prepared to perfection with only the best blends. But it would be a sacrilege to drink it on its own in a place like this. So why not order some tiramisu, a pastry, or the excellent house cake?

80 **PASTICCERIA ITALO DIDOVICH**

Campo Santa Marina 5908-5909 Castello ⑤
+39 041 523 0017

Despite being just a few minutes from Rialto, this historic pastry shop overlooks a rather small and quiet square, making it an excellent spot to sip some good coffee while seated outside. If you also want to munch on something, you'll be spoilt for choice with excellent sweet and savoury options.

5
HISTORIC CAFES

81 **SERRA DEI GIARDINI**
Viale Giuseppe Garibaldi 1254
Castello ⑤
+39 041 296 0360
serradeigiardini.org

While not technically a historic cafe, this greenhouse is the oldest place within the enclosure of the Biennale. Its exterior has been remarkably well preserved. The greenhouse still hosts various workshops and educational activities. There's also a flower shop where you can buy plants, and a cafe. A great place for a break during your visit to the arts festival.

82 **CAFFÈ FLORIAN**
Piazza San Marco 57
San Marco ①
+39 041 520 5641
caffeflorian.com

Caffè Florian has been here for over three hundred years, scrutinising the lives and fortunes of the noble families of the lagoon, from under the arcades in Piazza San Marco. Famous patrons include Casanova, Carlo Goldoni, Silvio Pellico, Lord Byron, Ugo Foscolo, Charles Dickens, Goethe, Rousseau, Gabriele d'Annunzio,... The only downside? The prices are definitely on the steep side.

82 CAFFÈ FLORIAN

83 HARRY'S BAR

Calle Vallaresso 1323
San Marco ①
+39 041 528 5777

Harry's Bar was founded in 1931, after an encounter between Giuseppe Cipriani (from Verona) and the American Harry Pickering. It has been very successful ever since. If you had stopped by in 1949, you might have spotted the writer Ernest Hemingway sitting at one of its tables. In 2001, Italy declared the restaurant a national monument. Their Bellini, which Arrigo Cipriani invented, is outstanding.

84 GRANCAFFÈ QUADRI

Piazza San Marco 121
San Marco ①
alajmo.it

As you stroll through the gilded and stuccoed rooms of Grancaffè Quadri, it's very easy to imagine the splendour of The Most Serene Republic during the 18th century. The coffee owes its name to its founder, Giorgio Quadri, who in 1775 founded the business with his wife and within a few years became famous for his coffee.

85 CAFFÈ LAVENA

Piazza San
Marco 133/134
San Marco ①
+39 041 522 4070
lavena.it

Carlo Lavena founded this wonderful place. Its main feature is the magnificent chandelier in the main hall. This was Richard Wagner's favourite *locale*, but it was equally popular with countless other musicians and writers.

GABRIELE GMEINER

65 PLACES TO SHOP

5 VINTAGE *alternatives* and SECONDHAND *shops*

86 **PENNY LANE SHOP**
Salizada
San Pantalon 39
San Polo ③
+39 041 524 4134
pennylaneshop.com

Established 10 years ago as a thrift shop, this tiny, well-stocked shop now also offers a selection of mainly new clothes from less common European brands, with an emphasis on quality and sustainability. They also carry a great range of colourful accessories from all over the world.

87 **L'ARMADIO DI COCO**
Calle de la
Vida 2516/A
San Marco ①
+39 041 241 3214
larmadiodicoco.com

L'Armadio di Coco is the place to go if timeless beauty and style are your thing. The vintage collection includes designer clothes, haute couture and rare and often almost impossible to find items. They also sell unique accessories and clothes by young designers and craftsmen.

88 **VINTAGERIA**
Campo S. Maria
Mater Domini 2120
San Polo ③
+39 348 825 6711
vintageria.it

If you're into eighties and nineties fashion, this place will make your heart sing. Vintageria sells a nice selection of pre-loved clothes, some of which are over thirty years old but which have withstood the test of time precisely because of their great quality. The fun website and e-shop are also worth checking out.

89 **LIBRERIA BERTONI**

Calle de la Mandola 3637/B
San Marco ①
+39 041 522 9583
bertonilibri.com

Walk with caution in this bookshop to avoid bumping into the many piles of books, some of which truly defy the laws of physics. There's a lot to browse, including rare volumes, paperbacks, new releases and discounted art books, which often go for half the price.

90 **USATA BY MARCO POLO**

Campo Santa Margherita 2915
Dorsoduro ②
+39 041 822 48 43
libreriamarcopolo.com

The newest addition to the Marco Polo team is this colourful little shop full of treasures waiting to be discovered. The selection of used books includes several Italian first editions of international classics, manuals that are out of print, art and cinema magazines and much more.

5 *fun*
OPEN-AIR MARKETS

91 **IL MERCATO DELL' ALTRAECONOMIA**
Rio Terà dei Pensieri
Santa Croce ③

This market is held every Thursday from 10.30 am to 6.30 pm. As the name suggests, this is not your typical market. The stallholders sell sustainable and ethical products, such as organic and locally grown food, medicinal plants and clothes produced with natural dyes.

92 **MERCATO DI RIO TERÀ SAN LEONARDO**
Strada Nova
Cannaregio ④

This small market is held in Strada Nova, off the Ponte delle Guglie bridge. It mostly has fruit and vegetable stalls, as well as smaller stalls that sell fish, and sometimes clothing and household goods. Open Monday through Saturday. The opening hours are the same as those of the local stores.

93 **MERCATO DI SACCA FISOLA**
Calle del Vaporetto 5
Giudecca ⑥

One of the only chances to see vehicles drive in Venice. Trucks are loaded with merchandise on the mainland, then ferried here where they open their doors and become street stalls. What do they sell? Extremely fresh food, as well as clothing and household items.

94 MERCATO DI VIA GARIBALDI

Via Garibaldi
Castello ⑤

Definitely the most popular market with locals, where Venetians outnumber the tourists. Here they sell fruit, vegetables, and fish. Open daily from 7 am to 2 pm.

95 ORTO DELLE MERAVIGLIE

AT: CARCERE FEMMINILE DELLA GIUDECCA (WOMEN'S PRISON)
Calle Convertite 712
Giudecca ⑥

A marvellous initiative of the Rio Terà dei Pensieri co-op. The Orto delle Meraviglie (Garden of Wonders) is a 6000-square-metre field, which is farmed by inmates of the women's prison, using organic methods only. They sell the fruits of their labour every week from a stall in Fondamenta del Carcere.

95 ORTO DELLE MERAVIGLIE

5 *extravagant*
BOOKSHOPS

96 LIBRERIA TOLETTA
Sacca della
Toletta 1214
Dorsoduro ②
+39 041 523 2034
latoletta.com

A historic bookstore which has an amazing collection of English-language books. It's also one of the largest in Venice. In 2008, Libreria Toletta started to publish its own books, with over 150 titles in its catalogue to date. Here you'll also find one of the city's premier literary cafes.

97 LIBRERIA BRUNO
Calle Lunga
San Barnaba 2729
Dorsoduro ②
+39 041 523 0379
b-r-u-n-o.it

The perfect bookshop for architects, designers, graphic designers, and creative minds in general, which sells a curated selection of magazines, which are difficult to find elsewhere. Here you'll find books spanning the worlds of art and design, as well as sociology, pedagogy, publishing and current affairs.

98 LIBRERIA ANTIQUARIA SEGNI NEL TEMPO
Calle Lunga
San Barnaba 2856
Dorsoduro ②
+39 041 722 909
maremagnum.com

Even if antique books aren't your thing, do visit this bookshop anyway if you enjoy a journey through the annals of Venetian history. In addition to stocking precious volumes and books you won't find anywhere else, the store also sells prints, maps of the city, and a variety of other printed curiosities.

99 LIBRERIA LINEA D'ACQUA

Calle della
Mandola 3717/D
San Marco ①
+39 041 522 4030
lineadacqua.it

Linea d'Acqua sells prints, antique books, and oil paintings of Venice, that highlight the ethereal beauty of the city. Step inside and you'll immediately be drawn to the large bookcase. Take a book, open it, inhale, and then nestle yourself in one of the two beautiful armchairs for a couple of hours.

100 LIBRERIA STUDIUM

Calle Larga 337
San Marco ①
+39 041 522 2382
libreriastudium.eu

One of the best reasons to visit this well-stocked bookshop, on two floors, near San Marco is its curated selection of books on Venice, with plenty of guides and books about the city's history. They also have lots of foreign language books, including an English, German and Spanish section.

97 LIBRERIA BRUNO

5 great places to buy GIFTS

101 I TRE MERCANTI
Campo de la Guerra 5364
Castello ⑤
+39 041 522 2901
itremercanti.it

In this shop you can buy excellent food and wine. In addition to bottles for all tastes and budgets, you'll also find homemade pasta of every variety here. The tiramisu to go, which they prepare in an open kitchen, is also excellent.

102 GIBERTO
Calle Caotorta 3565
San Marco ①
+39 041 277 0086
giberto.it

Where lies the boundary between craftsmanship and art? To what extent is a work the fruit of an artist's inspiration, and when does it simply express a way of being? These are the questions you will ask yourself as you gaze at refined and simple glass objects designed by Giberto Arrivabene Valenti Gonzaga. Make an appointment to visit the showroom.

103 MADERA
Campo San Barnaba 2762
Dorsoduro ②
+39 041 522 4181
maderavenezia.it

An original and elegant shop selling accessories, jewellery, and home decoration. The design of the products, which are made from everything from wood to plastic, is minimalist and contemporary. Shop here for a gift that has all the aesthetic allure of Venice with a contemporary twist.

104 **DAMOCLE EDIZIONI**

Calle del Perdon 1311
San Polo ③
+39 346 834 5720
edizionidamocle.wordpress.com

This tiny shop sells the publications of the eponymous indy publishing house. Browse their selection of original, refined books, including bilingual pocket-sized editions with beautifully designed book covers, handbound and illustrated art books, and elegant pamphlets that are handprinted with movable type.

105 **ATELIER CANESTRELLI**

Sacca della Toletta 1173
Dorsoduro ②
+39 041 277 0617
venicemirrors.com

Eclectic craftsman Stefano Coluccio finds inspiration in the history of art and in the works of the past masters to create unique mirrors with a convex shape, set in frames worked with gouache gilding. He loves to experiment and is constantly drawing on new research. No catalogue on the website, you'll have to visit the shop.

5 *inspiring*
CONCEPT STORES

106 **DECLARE**
Calle Seconda dei Saoneri 2671 B/C
San Polo ③
+39 041 822 3227
dclr.it

As you enter this concept store, you'll realise that even the smallest detail exudes a sense of refinement. It starts with the items on sale, including sophisticated leather bags and unusual publications, but even the atmosphere of this shop points to a keen interest in design and all things beautiful.

107 **TONOLO SELEZIONI**
Campo Santa Maria Formosa 5248/A
Castello ⑤
+39 041 241 1941
tonoloselezioni.com

In addition to the famous bags that are made from recycled truck tarps, you can find various items in this small concept store, including accessories, to home decoration and clothes, in black or white or combinations thereof, with a simple design.

108 **THE MERCHANT OF VENICE**
Campo San Fantin 1895
San Marco ①
+39 041 296 0559
themerchantofvenice.com

Venice played an important role in the history of perfumery. The Merchant of Venice concept store rekindles this history, selling eau de parfum and eau de toilette that recall the fragrances of the spice routes to the East, as well as a very popular line of home fragrances.

109 MALEFATTE VENEZIA

Fondamenta dei
Frari 2559/A
San Polo ③
+39 041 524 3125
malefattevenezia.it

This concept store sells T-shirts with colourful prints, bags and various items made from PVC, and a wide range of beauty products. Most surprisingly, however, all of these items are produced in Venetian prisons, under the supervision of the Rio Terà dei Pensieri cooperative.

110 SMALL CAPS

Campo Santa
Margherita 2916
Dorsoduro ②
+39 340 646 1841
smallcaps.it

Not a concept store per se. This graphic design workshop produces stunning posters, mainly with a Venetian theme and a refined design, in bright colours. A perfect example of how the creative excellence of Venice always succeeds in reinventing itself and standing out, while always remaining true to its values.

109 MALEFATTE VENEZIA

5 *stylish*
SHOE SHOPS

111 **ATELIER SEGALIN DI DANIELA GHEZZO**
Calle dei Fuseri 4365
San Marco ①
+39 041 522 2115
danielaghezzo.it

Time seems to have stopped in this deliciously eclectic workshop where craftsmanship reigns supreme. Here you will find footwear of every type and style. The models of the last century – which hang from the ceiling – are particularly fascinating. But the real selling point of this workshop are the bespoke shoes, which are real masterpieces, for anyone wishing to treat themselves to a one-of-a-kind shoe.

112 **PIEDÀTERRE**
Ruga dei Oresi 60
San Polo ③
+39 041 528 5513
piedaterre-venice.com

This colourful shop specialises in *le friulane*, or Venetian shoes. These shoes are in fact originally from Carnia, in the neighbouring region of Friuli (hence the name). They found their way to Venice after World War I, when a Friulian family began to sell them in Venice. They became popular with gondoliers and soon the rest of the city discovered them, too.

113 GIOVANNA ZANELLA

Calle de la Fava 5641
Castello ⑤
+39 041 523 5500
giovannazanella.com

Located just a few steps from the Rialto Bridge, Giovanna Zanella's workshop is where she produces her original creations. Her women's and men's shoes have eclectic shapes and colourful materials but all have in common that they are unique and one-of-a-kind.

114 GABRIELE GMEINER

Campiello del
Sol 951
San Polo ③
+39 338 896 2189
gabrielegmeiner.com

Entering the shop of cobbler Gabriele Gmeiner is like taking a journey back in time. The tools he uses to produce his elegant bespoke shoes hang on the wall. While these shoes are pricier than the mass-produced type, they are worth every penny.

115 QUORAMI

Calle della
Mandola 3730
San Marco ①
+39 041 241 3284
quorami.com

Country and western in Venice? Why not! Visit Giorgio, an expert leather craftsman, in his tiny shop and atelier where he produces his Texan-style designs as well as more classical styles. A great place to shop for shoes, belts, handbags and other accessories, all handmade and which can be customised on the spot.

5 *wonderful* ARTISAN TEXTILE *shops*

116 **CHIARASTELLA CATTANA**
Salizzada San Samuele 3216
San Marco ①
+39 041 522 4369
chiarastella cattana.com

This shop has a little bit of everything, including elegant fabrics for the home, as well as home accessories, glass objects and very occasionally some coveted items of clothing. Everything is designed and made in Italy.

118 FORTUNY SHOWROOM AND FACTORY

117 **TESSITURA BEVILACQUA**

Campiello de la Comare 1320
Santa Croce ③
+39 041 721566
luigi-bevilacqua.com

Venice's ability to turn out artisans in every discipline with unrivalled skills is truly incredible. The Bevilacqua family is just one example, creating precious velvets and silks, which are known and have been exported all over the world for many centuries. You'll even find their fabrics in the Kremlin.

118 **FORTUNY SHOWROOM AND FACTORY**

Fondamenta San Biagio 805
Giudecca ⑥
+39 393 825 7651
fortuny.com

Mariano Fortuny was an eclectic and cosmopolitan artist. In 1921, he bought an old convent on the island of Giudecca, converting it into a factory to produce his unique fabrics. Since then, production has continued. On weekends, you can visit the showroom and the beautiful garden, after booking.

119 **RUBELLI**
AT: CA' PISANI RUBELLI

Piscina S. Samuele 3393
San Marco ①
+39 041 523 6110
rubelli.com

Given its superb quality, the Rubelli showroom is almost like a museum, a crossroads of culture, where you can admire all the masterpieces of the history of this family of weaver. You can buy fabrics by the centimetre or the kilometre.

120 **CA' NOVA TESSUTI E TENDAGGI**

Campo San Luca 4264/A
San Marco ①
+39 041 520 3834
canovatessuti tendaggi.com

This historic shop sells a nice selection of international brands as well as brands that are designed and produced in Italy. Visit their showroom and immerse yourself in the dazzling array of colours and textures, of velvets, silk damasks, lampas, and many other traditional Venetian fabrics. Also a good place for home linens.

5 classy
HAUTE COUTURE
boutiques

121 **BARENA**
Calle Minelli 4260/B
San Marco ①
+39 041 523 8457
barenavenezia.com

This iconic shop sells refined classic apparel, with simple and elegant tailoring, for both women and men. They also stock a wide range of accessories such as shoes, perfumes, scarves, and hats. A good place to score a traditional cloak, the coat of preference of many Venetians in the past.

122 **LOUIS VUITTON**
Piazza San Marco 1345
San Marco ①
+39 041 522 4500
it.louisvuitton.com

It's true that many of the items you can buy here, while gorgeous, are not that different from what you would find in the shops in Paris or Tokyo. So what makes this shop so special? The surprising, small contemporary art gallery on the top floor hosts excellent rotating exhibitions. Worth the visit.

123 SARTORIA DEI DOGI

Calle del Tentor 1840
Santa Croce ③
+39 041 713 838
sartoriadeidogi.it

Sartoria dei Dogi (The Tailor of the Doges) is a small, family-owned shop that sells a contemporary take on traditional Venetian styles. The classic *tabarro* is transformed into an elegant and warm women's cape. They also sell colourful designs, which are all produced just a few kilometres from Venice.

124 DOLCE & GABBANA

Calle Larga XXII
Marzo 2188
San Marco ①
+39 041 520 9991
dolcegabbana.com

Everything Dolce & Gabbana designs is beautiful but there are no words to describe their new boutique. Calling Palazzo Torres a shop would almost be a slur. The building, which has been restored to its former glory, is a tribute to beauty.

125 MALLONI

Calle Frezzaria 1160
San Marco ①
+39 041 520 2115
malloni.com

As you walk through glittering Calle Frezzaria you will come upon the shop windows of Malloni. Their stylish, pure and eclectic designs definitely stand out among the crowd. And that is how this brand, which was established in 2000, gradually conquered the hearts of its loyal customer base: with innovative ideas, qualitative materials and an artisanal finish.

5 authentic Venetian MASK *and* CARNIVAL COSTUME SHOPS

126 CA' MACANA
Calle delle Boteghe 3172
Dorsoduro ②
+39 041 277 6142
camacana.com

Prepare to be overwhelmed by the riot of colour and shapes in this historic shop. On the right they have a wall of fame, of films and directors who have relied on this fantastic workshop for costumes. They also custom-decorate masks.

127 KARTARUGA IL CANOVACCIO
Calle delle Bande 5369-5370
Castello ⑤
+39 041 521 0393
kartaruga.it

The name of this historic Venetian workshop, which is a play on the words for 'paper' and 'turtle' in Italian, was inspired by the papier-mâché craze, the material that is traditionally used to produce masks, and the animal on the façade of their first workshop. Today Kartaruga collaborates with famous people and brands all over the world.

126 **CA' MACANA**

128 TRAGICOMICA

Calle dei
Nomboli 2800
San Polo ③
+39 041 721 102
tragicomica.it

You'll find this wonderful mask shop opposite Goldoni's house. Here they proudly uphold the tradition of the *maschereri*, the artisans who have been practising the art of mask making since the 15th century. While there are plenty of shops that sell masks in Venice, Tragicomica is one of the few that also produces them.

129 NICOLAO ATELIER

Fondamenta
Misericordia 2590
Cannaregio ④
+39 041 520 7051
nicolao.com

It's worth visiting this workshop just for the fairy-tale atmosphere inside. Nicolao sells carnival costumes, sequined fabrics, masks, of the highest workmanship, supplying clothes and costumes for famous characters in countless theatres around the world.

130 ALBERTO SARRIA MASKS

Ruga Vecchia San
Giovanni 777
San Polo ③
+39 041 520 7278
masksvenice.com

The founder's children have been managing this workshop for many years, selling papier-mâché masks. They also sell leather-goods, porcelain and puppets. The masks represent the characters of the Venetian tradition, but there are also some exceptions. Don't hesitate to ask the staff if you have a special request.

5 *shops for people who value* HANDWRITTEN LETTERS

131 PAOLO OLBI

Calle Foscari 3253/A
Dorsoduro ②
+39 041 523 7655
olbi.atspace.com

Paolo Olbi creates marbled paper and leather-bound books. He works according to the centuries-old Venetian tradition. While his designs are respectful of tradition, he always adds a modern, original twist. A wonderful place for an authentic Venetian gift.

132 ALBERTO VALESE – EBRU

Campo Santo Stefano 347
San Marco ①
+39 041 523 8830
albertovalese-ebru.it

In Turkish, *ebru* literally means 'cloudy'. The term describes the process, used by Alberto Valdese, to create magnificent multicoloured works that imitate the veining of marble or the changing colours of the clouds. He usually works on paper, but the shop also sells artefacts in silk, wood and other materials.

135 GIANNI BASSO STAMPATORE

133 PAPEROOWL

Calle Longa 2155/A
Santa Croce ③
+39 041 476 1974
paperoowl.com

A pretty little shop and workshop that, in addition to the usual handmade works of paper, sells jewellery made from this incredibly versatile material. The 'Venice in a box' collection is also fun. This three-dimensional postcard features a small outline of the city.

134 CHARTA

Calle dei Fabbri 831
San Marco ①
+39 041 522 9801
chartaonline.com

Book lovers will go crazy at Charta, which sells collectible books with unique bindings, excellent quality prints, and bizarre objects of all kinds. Bear in mind that the shop is also a workshop so it may be closed during the day.

135 GIANNI BASSO STAMPATORE

Calle del Fumo 5306
Cannaregio ④
+39 041 523 4681

The Gutenberg of Venice. This incredible craftsman prints all his works by hand. The shop is packed with old machines and strewn with type cases, bookplates, handwritten letters, illustrations, and business cards. He displays the business cards he produced for some of his most famous clients, from Hugh Grant to Ryuichi Sakamoto in his shop window.

5
OPTICIANS
that sell original frames

136 OTTICA URBANI

Bocca di Piazza 1280
San Marco ①
+39 041 522 4140
otticaurbani.com

If you're a designer, architect, artist, creative mind, or if you simply love things that are well-executed, then this is the optician for you. This is not just a shop, but a workshop that designs and produces original models, combining experimentation and innovative materials with care and craftsmanship.

137 L'ALTRAOTTICA

Calle Lunga Santa
Maria Formosa 6206
Castello ⑤
+39 041 241 1856
laltraottica.com

This tiny shop sells designer frames by some of the world's most famous brands. In 2008, they also launched their own brand, using natural materials only and creating a line of very light and extremely wearable wooden and bamboo frames. Over time, the frame adapts to the wearer's face, becoming completely exclusive.

138 MICROMEGA OTTICA

Calle delle
Ostreghe 2436
San Marco ①
+39 041 296 0765
micromegaottica.com

Micromega Ottica sells a range of interesting frames, which are designed and crafted by the owners in their Venetian workshop. Their trademark: frames in titanium, which are assembled without glue and without screws, with laser-cut lenses, and which weigh nextto nothing.

139 OTTICA MANUELA

Salizzada San
Samuele 3145
San Marco ①
+39 041 521 0268

This small eyewear shop is famous for its frames which are arranged and exhibited like tiny contemporary masterpieces. And in fact, that is exactly what they are, as these original and distinctive frames are real eye-catchers because of their innovative shapes and material. A place where everyone will find a frame that suits his or her personality, largely thanks to the owner's perspicacity.

140 OTTICA CARRARO

Calle de la
Mandola 3706
San Marco ①
+39 041 520 4258
otticacarraro.it

Some new eyewear as a souvenir? Why not? You'll definitely find something to your liking here in the colourful selection at Carraro. Most of the frames are made from cellulose acetate, produced from cotton flakes, which is very durable and free of toxic components.

136 OTTICA URBANI

5
JEWELLERS
for all tastes

141 **PALWER**

Salizzada San Samuele 3359
San Marco ①
+39 041 528 5435
palwer.com

The designer Alessandro Palwer sells jewellery that is both classically elegant but has an unmistakable, contemporary style. Rose gold, hammered gold, and blackened gold, as well as brown diamonds and emeralds are just some of the materials he uses in his very diverse but always tasteful and refined collections.

142 **MAISON 203 VE**

Ruga Vecchia San Giovanni 419
San Polo ③
+39 041 522 8379
maison203.com

An interesting boutique that sells jewellery designed with hi-tech imaging and produced with a 3D printer. As you can imagine, the design is most definitely innovative. They also strongly believe in good workmanship, however, which is why all the jewellery is hand-finished. They use everything from synthesised nylon to brass.

143 OHMYBLUE

Campo San
Tomà 2865
San Polo ③
+39 041 243 5741
ohmyblue.com

OHMYBLUE is more of an art gallery than a jeweller's. All the items here are designed by artists and designers. The shapes are eclectic and the style unusual. They also sell home decoration and clothing.

144 NICOTRA DI SAN GIACOMO VENEZIA

Calle del
Tagliapietra 2587
San Polo ③
+39 041 275 9432
ndsg.it

'Weavers of jewellery' is what we call the artisans at Nicotra. This small shop specialises in fluid, flexible jewellery. They weave gold and silver into a tight weave with silk yarns to produce designs that adapt to the wearer's body, like a bespoke suit.

145 MATERIALMENTE

Merceria San
Salvador 4850
San Marco ①
+39 041 528 6881
*materialmente
venezia.com*

This small shop exudes all the charm of an unknown underwater universe. Strange sea creatures made of steel and glass hover over the jewellery collection, with its fleeting, almost esoteric designs. The artists Maddalena Venier and Alessandro Salvadori produce unique and timeless designs.

5 *workshops* *for creations with* **GLASS** *and* **VENETIAN PEARLS**

146 DAVIDE PENSO
Fondamenta
Riva Longa 48
Murano ⑦
+39 041 739 819
davidepenso.com

What better place to find glass objects than Murano, where this art form was born? Davide Penso is one of the most illustrious representatives of this craft, having exhibited his work in some of the most important Venetian and international museums. He has collaborated with many leading brands and lectures at various prestigious institutions.

146 DAVIDE PENSO

147 GOTO MURANO PROJECT

Merceria
Orologio 257
San Marco ①
+39 324 587 1619
gotomurano.com

There is more to the '*goto de fornasa*' or *fornasa* glass than meets the eye. Originally these handmade glasses were the first test to which apprentices were subjected, requiring them to create a personalised glass. GOTO is an entrepreneurial project that focusses on uniqueness and wisdom, values that you will encounter in all the items they sell.

148 GENNINGER STUDIO

Campiello
Barbaro 364
Dorsoduro ②
+39 041 522 5565
genningerstudio.com

Earrings, bracelets and necklaces aren't the only things you'll spot in the studio of designer Leslie Ann Genninger. She also sells chandeliers, glasses and other gadgets, which she produces with master glassmakers who use a technique that goes back a thousand years.

149 VENETIAN DREAMS

Calle de la
Mandola 3805/A
San Marco ①
+39 041 523 0292
marisaconvento.it

Marisa Convento is the most famous Venetian *impiraressa*, the word for a woman who makes glass jewellery beads. Everyone in Venice knows her, because she also actively contributes to initiatives to promote hidden gems and little-known artisanal treasures. Her creations are simply magnificent.

150 MARINA E SUSANNA SENT

Campo San Vio 669
Dorsoduro ②
+39 041 520 8136
*marinae
susannasent.com*

The Sent sisters transform glass into anything and every shape imaginable, whether ethereal or material. They sell jewellery in the form of soap bubbles, corals and even tribal artefacts, made from this glittering material.

FONDAZIONE QUERINI STAMPALIA

45 BUILDINGS TO ADMIRE

5 great buildings by
PALLADIO

151 **BASILICA DEL REDENTORE**
Campo del Santissimo Redentore
Giudecca ⑥
+39 041 275 0462
chorusvenezia.org

Palladio was commissioned to build the basilica of the Redentore (Redeemer) by the Venetian Senate, to celebrate the end of the terrible plague epidemic that struck the city in 1577. This refined building has harmonious proportions and is home to paintings by artists such as Palma il Giovane, Tintoretto, and Paolo Veronese.

151 BASILICA DEL REDENTORE

152 CHURCH OF SAN FRANCESCO DELLA VIGNA

Ramo Al Ponte
San Francesco
Castello ⑤
+39 041 523 5341
isevenezia.it

The church owes its name to the vineyard that stood here before the church was built. It dates back to the 16th century and was designed by Sansovino. It was Palladio, however, who, many years later, created the elegant façade. The design of the imposing central window recalls the windows of ancient Roman baths.

153 BASILICA DI SAN GIORGIO MAGGIORE

Isola di San
Giorgio Maggiore ⑥
+39 041 522 7827

The church was designed by Palladio in the late stages of his career. The project was inspired by the shapes of the ancient Roman thermal baths, which the architect studied during his travels. The result is a solemn and airy space, which Vasari also admired.

154 CONVENTO DELLA CARITÀ

AT: GALLERIE DELL' ACCADEMIA

Campo della
Carità 1050
Dorsoduro ②
+39 041 522 2247
gallerieaccademia.it

Today, the Accademia is one of Venice's most important museum, housing extraordinary artworks such as Leonardo da Vinci's *Vitruvian Man* and Giorgione's *The Tempest*. Originally, however, this was a church and convent, whose renovation was entrusted to Palladio. Only the eastern wing of the cloister survived to this day in its original form.

155 CHURCH OF SANTA MARIA DELLA PRESENTAZIONE

Fondamenta delle
Zitelle 33
Giudecca ⑤
+39 041 309 6605

The Church of S.M. della Presentazione, which the locals call Le Zitelle (Old Maids), is part of a Jesuit complex, which gave shelter to young women without a dowry (hence the name). The attribution to Palladio is disputed. However many details link it to other works of him.

5 places to admire CARLO SCARPA'*s work*

156 **FONDAZIONE QUERINI STAMPALIA**
Campo Santa Maria Formosa 5252
Castello ⑤
+39 041 271 1411
querinistampalia.org

This foundation hosts art and photography exhibitions, and much more. But this really doesn't do justice to the architecture of details, by its architect, Carlo Scarpa. One of Italy's most famous contemporary architects, the master supervised every single inch and detail on which you will feast your eyes.

157 **NEGOZIO OLIVETTI**
Piazza San Marco 101
San Marco ①
+39 041 522 8387
negoziolivetti.it

Scarpa often said he was a Byzantine at heart, and this little gem, which is tucked away in the arcades of Piazza San Marco, shows exactly why. Check out the unusual decorative elements: the wonderful central staircase, the richness of the materials, and the refinement of every detail.

158 **SCULPTURE GARDEN, PADIGLIONE ITALIA**
AT: GIARDINI DELLA BIENNALE
Castello ⑤
+39 041 521 8711
labiennale.org

Venice's Giardini della Biennale are famous for the art exhibitions that are held there, as well as for the famous names that designed each pavilion, from Giò Ponti to Stirling. Scarpa's sculpture garden, inside the central Padiglione Italia, is a must-see. Enjoy a moment of peace and meditation.

159 AULA BARATTO

AT: UNIVERSITÀ CA' FOSCARI
Campo San Sebastiano 1686
Dorsoduro ②
+39 041 234 7311
unive.it

An excellent example of a modern addition to a historical building, the Baratto Auditorium is a beautiful illustration of the maestro's modus operandi, as it was created in collaboration with Venetian artisan workshops. The Ca' Foscari University organises guided tours of the building. Contact *cafoscaritour@unive.it* for bookings.

160 IUAV UNIVERSITY-TOLENTINI

Fondamenta dei Tolentini 191
Santa Croce ③
iuav.it

This project, which was completed after Scarpa's death, shows how the architect always liked to think out of the box. He dismantled the old doorway in the façade, which previously served as a gate, and used it as a basin in his design, replacing it with a sliding gate made from iron and Istrian stone.

5 BASILICAS *you should see*

161 **BASILICA DI SAN PIETRO DI CASTELLO**
Calle Seconda
de la Fava 70
Castello ⑤
+39 041 275 0462
chorusvenezia.org

Like so many other Venetian churches, this basilica is the result of the stratification of multiple additions and layers, from the 9th century AD onwards. The best-known architectural intervention is that of Palladio, to whom the building is attributed. Today it has a Latin cross plan with three naves, and a tripartite façade.

162 **BASILICA DEI SANTI GIOVANNI E PAOLO**
Campo dei
Santi Giovanni
e Paolo 6363
Castello ⑤
+39 041 523 5913
basilicasantigiovanniepaolo.it

As is often the case in Venice, it's difficult to establish a hierarchical list of all the precious artworks that are preserved in this huge brick edifice, which the locals call San Zanipolo. In random order, they include the *Saint Vincent Ferrer Altarpiece* by Bellini, Vivarini's polychrome stained-glass window, the magnificent cycle of frescoes by Veronese. But there's much more.

162 BASILICA DEI SANTI GIOVANNI E PAOLO

163 **BASILICA DI SANTA MARIA DELLA SALUTE**

Fondamenta Salute 1
Dorsoduro ②
+39 041 274 3928
basilicasalutevenezia.it

Like the Basilica of the Redentore, this church was also built as an ex-voto offering to the Virgin Mary as a sign of gratitude after a terrible plague epidemic. The commission was entrusted to Baldassare Longhena, who – borrowing many solutions from Palladio – designed one of the most prestigious examples of baroque architecture in Venice.

164 **BASILICA DEI SANTI MARIA E DONATO**

Calle San Donato 11
Murano ⑦
+39 041 739 056
sandonatomurano.it

Dating back to the 7th century, this basilica has two side aisles, which are supported by Greek marble columns and Byzantine capitals. The precious floor mosaics, made from marble and glass paste, represent geometric decorations and mythological animals, and were produce circa 1140.

165 **CHURCH OF SANTA MARIA ASSUNTA**

Fondamenta dei Borgognoni 24
Torcello ⑨
+39 041 730 084

The basilica of Torcello is a simple brick building. Construction started in the year 639 AD. Its bell tower is the point of reference for the whole northern lagoon. The interior is famous for the precious mosaics made of gold leaf, depicting *The Apotheosis of Christ* and *The Last Judgment*.

5 addresses to discover
CELEBRITIES OF THE PAST

166 PALAZZO MOCENIGO
Salizada San Stae 1992
Santa Croce ③
+39 041 721798
mocenigo.visitmuve.it

Palazzo Mocenigo belonged to the Mocenigo family from the 17th until the 20th century, when the last descendant bequeathed it to the city of Venice. Lord Byron lived here for three years, from 1816, where he studied Armenian, Italian and the Venetian dialect. Here he also wrote his drama *Manfred* and other famous works.

167 PALAZZO GIUSTINIAN
Calle Giustinian 3228
Dorsoduro ②

Built in the 15th century by the Giustinian family, one of the most eminent families in renaissance Venice. Wagner stayed there for seven months in 1858, during his first visit to the lagoon. Here he also composed *Tristan und Isolde*.

169 **PALAZZO FORTUNY**

168 CASA DI CARLO GOLDONI

Calle del Scaleter 2794
San Polo ③
+39 041 275 9325
carlogoldoni. visitmuve.it

Goldoni is one of the most famous Venetian playwrights of all time. Today his 'home in the lagoon' has become a museum dedicated to him, showcasing a collection of documents, images, portraits, and... puppets. The highlight of the collection however is the small puppet theatre of the Grimani ai Servi family, with thirty puppets in elaborate 18th-century clothes.

169 PALAZZO FORTUNY

Calle Traghetto Vecchio 3958
San Marco ①
+39 041 520 0995
fortuny.visitmuve.it

Mariano Fortuny Madrazo was an eclectic artist, a painter, an engraver, and a set designer. He also designed textiles and fashion and founded the Fortuny textile company, which still produces printed fabrics today using traditional methods. It's thanks to him that the city of Venice has a Fortuny Museum, a splendid contemporary art space in the 15th-century building that he renovated and elected to make his home.

170 COLLEZIONE PEGGY GUGGENHEIM

AT: PALAZZO VENIER DEI LEONI
Calle San Cristoforo 701-704
Dorsoduro ②
+39 041 240 5411
guggenheim-venice.it

Palazzo Venier dei Leoni is an unfinished building, which was started in 1748, by Lorenzo Boschetto, who also designed the Church of San Barnaba in Venice. In 1948, Peggy Guggenheim, a famous intellectual and art patron, bought the palazzo and lived there for the next thirty years. Today it is a modern art museum, run by the Guggenheim Foundation, and a must-see.

5 VILLAS at the LIDO of Venice

171 **VILLINO MON PLAISIR**
Granviale Santa Maria Elisabetta 14
Lido di Venezia ⑧

A small, early 20th-century villa, this irregularly shaped building, which is decorated with porcelain and wrought iron, bears all the hallmarks of the typical architecture of this period in the Lido: a curious collection of archetypes ranging from Venetian shapes to elements that were inspired by the works of the Austrian architect Joseph Hoffman.

172 **VILLA OTELLO**
Via Dandolo 22
Lido di Venezia ⑧

The design of Villa Otello is neo-Gothic and neo-byzantine, with art deco elements. The façade features a sequence of mullioned windows decorated with capitals and slender columns. The fine workmanship of the wrought-iron gate, one of the few to survive successive wars unscathed, is also noteworthy.

173 **VILLINO GEMMA**
Via Dardanelli 22
Lido di Venezia ⑧

An elegant building with eclectic decorations. The villa's façade features a painted majolica band on the first floor, and frescos of female figures in the attic.

174 VILLINO DELLE FATE

Via Dardanelli 50
Lido di Venezia ⑧

The 'villa of the fairies' is a small building, which was built in 1914 from plastered bricks, while the finishes and decorations use exposed brick. Note the colour combinations and the turret that juts out from the side of the central volume.

175 VILLA EVA

Granviale Santa Maria Elisabetta 49
Lido di Venezia ⑧

Villa Eva features references to the art nouveau style and classical elements of the Renaissance. It has an imposing façade with a tympanum, as well as floral decorations and mosaics with allegorical representations.

174 VILLINO DELLE FATE

The 5 most beautiful **PALAZZOS** *along the Canal Grande*

176 **PALAZZO LOREDAN VENDRAMIN**
Calle Larga
Vendramin 2040
Cannaregio ④
+39 041 276 0407
casinovenezia.it

Designed by architect Mauro Codussi and built between the 14th and 15th century, this palace is one of the most representative buildings of the Venetian Renaissance. The tripartite façade is an example of balance and proportion, combining stringcourses and the three superimposed architectural orders Doric, Ionic, and Corinthian. Today the building is home to the Venice Casino.

177 **CA' D'ORO**
Fondamenta
Trapolin 3932
Cannaregio ④
+39 041 522 2349
cadoro.org

Ca' d'Oro must have been resplendent when it was first built in the 15th century, with its triumphant polychrome marbles and gold-leaf decorations (hence the name). This gem would have been lost for posterity, if the art patron Giorgio Franchetti hadn't saved it from decay.

178 **PALAZZO GRASSI**
Campo San
Samuele 3231
San Marco ①
+39 041 200 157
palazzograssi.it

Palazzo Grassi was one of the last palaces to be built on the Canal Grande before the fall of the Most Serene Republic of Venice. Today this amazing museum complex is home to François Pinault's contemporary art collection.

179 CA' FOSCARI

Calle Larga
Foscari 3246
Dorsoduro ②
+39 041 234 8111
unive.it

This is probably the best lookouts along the Canal Grande, as its location along the widening bend offers a sweeping view, from the Gallerie dell'Accademia to the Rialto Bridge. This impressive, late-15th-century palace is now home to Ca' Foscari University. You can visit the period rooms by appointment.

180 CA' PESARO

Fondamenta de
Ca' Pesaro 2076
Santa Croce ③
+39 041 721 127
capesaro.visitmuve.it

A magnificent example of the Venetian Baroque, this palazzo once belonged to the Pesaro family and was designed by the architect Baldassarre Longhena. The façade is an imposing *chiaroscuro* of statues and bas-reliefs, while the interior is magnificently decorated by Giovanni Battista Pittoni. It is also home to the International Gallery of Modern Art.

177 CA' D'ORO

5 CONFRATERNITY BUILDINGS *of Venice's Scuole Grandi*

181 SCUOLA GRANDE DI SAN MARCO

Campo dei
Santi Giovanni e
Paolo 6777
Castello ⑤
+39 041 529 4323
*scuolagrande
sanmarco.it*

A good building to understand how exceptional Venice really is. The polychrome marbles and the trompe l'oeil of the façade conceal the entrance to the city's hospital! The lavish salon is lined with ancient books of medicine and bizarre surgical instruments from the last century. The phantasmagorical inlaid ceiling alone is worth the visit.

181 SCUOLA GRANDE DI SAN MARCO

182 SCUOLA GRANDE DI SANTA MARIA DELLA MISERICORDIA

Fondamenta
Misericordia 3599
Cannaregio ④
+39 337 144 0557
misericordiadivenezia.it

During the heyday of the *Serenissima*, the city's confraternities were lay associations that performed acts of charity and whose members were prominent citizens. The seat of the Misericordia was designed by Jacopo Sansovino in the 16th century. The building has now been restored to its former glory and hosts events and exhibitions.

183 SCUOLA GRANDE DEI CARMINI

Calle de la
Scuola 2616-2617
Dorsoduro ②
+39 041 528 9420
scuolagrandecarmini.it

The Scuola Grande dei Carmini was built by Baldassare Longhena in the 17th century, and lovely to behold, with its chiselled marble floors, stuccoes and inlaid ceilings. The chapter hall features nine beautiful paintings by Giambattista Tiepolo. Definitely worth seeing.

184 SCUOLA GRANDE SAN GIOVANNI EVANGELISTA

Campiello de
la Scuola 2454
San Polo ③
+39 041 718 234
scuolasangiovanni.it

If, during your peregrinations, you happen to spot a magnificent marble arch that draws you in, then walk through it. The arch, by Pietro Lombardo, is the entrance to the complex of the Scuola Grande San Giovanni Evangelista, a magnificent building that houses works by Giambattista Tiepolo and Palma Vecchio.

185 SCUOLA DI SAN GIORGIO DEGLI SCHIAVONI

Calle Furlani 3259/A
Castello ⑤
+39 041 522 8828
scuoladalmata venezia.com

This confraternity is linked to the Dalmatian community (called the 'slaves' – *schiavoni* – i.e. the Slavs, hence the name) and is the only one that is still in operation to this day. The highlight is the small room with a wonderful cycle of frescoes by Carpaccio, dating back to the 1500s.

5
SYNAGOGUES
hidden in the Ghetto

186 **THE SPANISH SYNAGOGUE**
Calle Ghetto
Vecchio 1147
Cannaregio ④
+39 041 715 359
museoebraico.it

Like all the synagogues in the ghetto, this synagogue occupies the top part of an existing building, to bypass the ban on building new places of worship. So it's not immediately recognisable from the outside, although the colourful glass windows on the façade hint at the rich decorations inside. The synagogue can only be visited during the six winter months.

187 **LEVANTINE SYNAGOGUE**
Calle Ghetto
Vecchio 1154
Cannaregio ④
+39 041 715 359
museoebraico.it

The Levantine synagogue, like the others in the ghetto, belongs to communities that came from all over Europe and, having settled in Venice, created a place of worship to maintain and preserve their rituals. Unlike the Spanish synagogue, it's only open during the summer, which is when celebrations are halted.

188 SCUOLA GRANDE TEDESCA

Campo di Ghetto Nuovo 2902/B
Cannaregio ④
+39 041 715 012

The German synagogue was the first to be built in the Jewish ghetto. It dates from 1527, although the decorations were heavily reworked in the late baroque period. In the 19th century, its position and orientation were altered for structural reasons. The synagogue, like all the others in the ghetto, can be visited during a guided tour by the Jewish Museum of Venice.

189 SCOLA CANTON

Calle Orto 1191
Cannaregio ④
+39 041 715 012
jvenice.org

What makes the Scola Canton so unique, compared with all the other synagogues in the ghetto, is the presence of eight wooden panels that depict episodes from the Bible. It is located in the corner building of the square and is easy to spot with its small wooden dome.

190 ITALIAN SYNAGOGUE

Calle Ghetto Vecchio 2883
Cannaregio ④
+39 041 715 012
jvenice.org

The Italian synagogue is the smallest of the five synagogues in Venice, and was dedicated to the Jewish community of Venice. It's also the simplest and the most barren of the five. It shares its entrance with some private dwellings. While the interior is rather simple it is also extremely luminous thanks to the five large windows that give out onto the square.

5 *examples of* GREAT CONTEMPORARY ARCHITECTURE

191 **CEMETERY OF SAN MICHELE**
Isola San Michele ⑦
+39 041 729 2841

Architects will be interested to know that the extension of the historic cemetery of Venice was designed by the British architect David Chipperfield. Everybody else might find it fascinating that personalities such as Emilio Vedova, Stravinsky, and Christian Doppler, are buried here. In either case, it's worth a visit.

192 **TEATRINO DI PALAZZO GRASSI**
AT: PALAZZO GRASSI
Campo San Samuele 3231
San Marco ①
+39 041 523 1680
palazzograssi.it

The architect Tadao Ando designed the space of this small theatre, with curves of cement and marble, using the vibrating and zenithal light to expand the space. The hall seats an audience of 225 and offers a nice programme of events including concerts, conferences, shows, and projections.

193 **FORMER CHURCH OF SANTA MARTA**
Calle Dietro Ai Magazzini
Dorsoduro ②
comune.venezia.it

After a fantastic restoration by the architects Vittorio De Feo and Vincenzo Casali, this Romanesque building with brickwork and trusses now features an elegant wooden reversible structure, that is used as an exhibition hall and theatre.

194 FONDAZIONE VEDOVA

Fondamenta Zattere
Ai Saloni 50
Dorsoduro ②
+39 041 522 6626
fondazionevedova.org

The works of the great artist Emilio Vedova could not have been placed in a more suggestive location. This former salt warehouse has brick walls and an austere architecture. The architect Renzo Piano's idea to install and use a track system with mechanical arms to hang and move the artworks is quite interesting.

195 FONDAZIONE CINI

AT: LE STANZE DEL VETRO / THE GLASS ROOMS
Isola di San Giorgio Maggiore 8
Isola di san Giorgio Maggiore ⑥
+39 041 522 9138
lestanzedelvetro.org

The island of San Giorgio is definitely worth a visit for all the treasures it hides, including the glass rooms by the architect Annabelle Selldorf. This stark, minimalist space is dedicated to the study and exhibition of contemporary artistic Venetian glass.

195 FONDAZIONE CINI

TERRACE OF FONDACO DEI TEDESCHI

95 PLACES TO DISCOVER IN VENICE

5

WORDS *to get around Venice*

196 **CALLE**

By *calle* we mean the street between two continuous rows of buildings. There may be some variations, depending on the characteristics of the street itself: the *callesel* refers to a street that is very narrow (up to sixty centimetres wide) *ramo* is used for a dead end, and *salizada* if the street is somehow important.

197 **CAMPO**

Campi and *campielli* – depending on their size – are what we call 'squares', the true centre of Venetian social life. Some of these feature a stone wellhead, to protect the opening. Today they are all sealed, but at one time they were the only source of drinking water.

198 **FONDAMENTA**

A *fondamenta* is a street that runs along a canal; it can have a railing (but not necessarily) and can be covered with a portico, in which case it's called a *sotoportego*. Many *fondamente* also have *approdi* or docks, steps made of Istrian stone to help people get in and out of boats.

199 **CORTE**

As with the campo, the *corte* (courtyard) is comprised of an empty space surrounded by homes. However, while the '*campo*', as a square, has a more public and social dimension, the *corte* refers to a smaller sphere of interactions, limited to the inhabitants of the homes that surround it.

200 **RIO**

The *rio* is a smaller version of a canal, and a key element to understand the road system of Venice's historic centre. Some of them trace the path of ancient lagoon channels. Others, which generally have a straightened path, are totally artificial.

5 less crowded
ALTERNATIVES TO 'STRADA NOVA'

201 **FONDAMENTA DEI MORI**
Cannaregio ④

This *fondamenta*, which runs parallel to Strada Nova, is an excellent idea for a walk without all the tourist chaos. In Campo dei Mori there's a good tavern, and a statue of Signor Rioba. Walk on and you'll run into Tintoretto's house, which is marked by a plaque.

202 **CAMPIELLO DELLA SCUOLA**
San Polo ③

If you need to get from Rialto to the train station, a good alternative to Strada Nova is to walk down the narrow streets of San Polo. Pass through Campiello della Scuola, and you'll see the Scuola Grande San Giovanni Evangelista on one side and a church of the same name on the other.

203 CAMPO SAN GIACOMO DELL'ORIO

San Polo ③

Another idea to get from Rialto to the train station is to follow the Canal Grande. Walking through the Ruga degli Oresi, for example, you'll come across a series of pretty shops. Then head to Campo San Cassiano, where you can visit the church, and finally cross Campo San Giacomo dell'Orio, which is still an authentically Venetian neighbourhood.

204 CAMPO DEI FRARI

San Polo ③

There are plenty of excellent opportunities to discover the beauty of Venice as you stroll through the heart of San Polo. Walk up Ramo Cimesin and follow Campo dei Frari, to see three highlights of Venice's artistic heritage in rapid succession. They are the Church and Scuola Grande (confraternity) of San Rocco and the Basilica dei Frari. What's more, you can also take a gondola across the Canal Grande in this neighbourhood.

205 FONDAMENTA SANTA CATERINA

Cannaregio ④

The northeast side of Cannaregio also has some interesting gems in store for you, and is almost always deserted. For instance, by walking down Fondamenta Santa Caterina, you will run into the church of the same name, and then Palazzo Zeno. Moving on to the right, on Campo dei Gesuiti, the Crociferi cloister is an excellent excuse to stop for a break and a spritz.

207 CASINO ZANE

5 ancient **CASINI** (boudoirs) open to the public

206 CASINO VENIER
Ponte dei
Baretteri 4939
San Marco ①
+39 041 522 7079
afvenezia.it

The Casino Venier is probably the most fascinating of the casini that are still open to the public. Its 18th-century look and feel has been preserved intact, with marbles, stuccoes, and original mirrors. In the entrance hall there is a peephole hidden in the floor, from which you could spy on whomever was at the front door, without being seen. The Casino Venier became the headquarters of the Alliance Française in 1987.

207 CASINO ZANE
AT: PALAZZETTO BRU ZANE
Campiello del Forner
o del Marangon 2368
San Polo ③
+39 041 521 1005
bru-zane.com

This casino was built at the end of the 17th century to a design by Baldassarre Longhena's workshop, and conceived as a place of leisure for the Zane Palace, just a few steps away. This meeting point for the aristocracy was lavishly decorated by various Venetian artisans. Thanks to a major restoration, it has been restored to its original splendour.

208 CASINO SAGREDO

Campo Santa
Sofia 4198/99
Cannaregio ④
+39 041 241 3111
casagredohotel.com

This gorgeous casino has six sumptuous rooms, covered in painted stuccoes and bas-reliefs, including frescoes by Giambattista Tiepolo and Pietro Longhi. Nowadays it's become a hotel, so visiting it is not always easy, but even just popping in and walking through the main staircase, by Andrea Tirali, is worth your while.

209 CASINO DANDOLO

Calle Vallaresso 1332
San Marco ①
+39 041 520 0211
hotelmonaco.it

The Casino Dandolo, also known as 'Il Ridotto' (The Private Room) is now located inside the Hotel Monaco, on the main floor of the building, and consists of a magnificent hall surrounded by eight rooms. The palace belonged to the Dandolo family, but in 1638 it became the property of the State, which turned it into a gambling house, Il Ridotto.

210 CASINO DI PALAZZO CORNER CONTARINI DEI CAVALLI

Ramo de le
Muneghe 3980
San Marco ①

The casino of Palazzo Corner Contarini dei Cavalli is definitely a hidden secret. Built around 1450, this building is now used as an office building by the Ministry of Justice. Ask to enter, and you may find yourself in a room with shelves and shelves of Dutch pottery, depicting mills, animals and quaint houses.

5 places featured in CORTO MALTESE's *comic book*

211 PONTE WIDMAN
Cannaregio ④

Giovanni Widman, a German of humble extraction, arrived in Venice in 1590, where he earned a fortune, leading his descendants to hold prestigious positions in Venice and beyond. The bridge that is named after him is located near Campo dei Miracoli. In the tales of Corto Maltese, it is called the Bridge of Nostalgia.

211 PONTE WIDMAN

212 CORTE BOTERA

Calle Vesier
Castello ⑤

All of the adventurer Corto Maltese's wanderings around the world start from Corte Botera, which in the story is called the *corte sconta detta arcana* (hidden courtyard also referred to as mysterious). It's a small and charming square with a well, a narrow staircase, and a balcony full of flowers.

213 TITIAN'S WORKSHOP

Calle Tiziano 5182
Cannaregio ④

The home of the famous painter became the home of Corto Maltese, the globetrotter character of Hugo Pratt's comic books. Unfortunately, nowadays it's not open to the public and little suggests that great minds have passed through here, except for a stone plaque that attests to their presence.

214 HUGO PRATT'S HOUSE

Via Doge Galla 21
Lido di Venezia ⑧

Pratt lived abroad for most of his adult life. His mother resided in Malamocco however and the author would occasionally spend some time there.

215 DA SCARSO

Piazzale Malamocco 5
Lido di Venezia ⑧
+39 041 770 834
trattoriadascarso.it

Hugo Pratt mentions this rustic restaurant, located in the ancient village of Malamocco, in 'The Angel at the Window of the East'. This is an excellent idea for an outdoor lunch in a different setting, as the garden is decorated with shells and fishing nets.

5

PANORAMIC VIEWS
of Venice

216 **TERRACE OF FONDACO DEI TEDESCHI**

Calle del Fontego dei Tedeschi
San Marco ①
+39 041 314 2000
dfs.com

The splendid panoramic terrace on the roof of the Fondaco dei Tedeschi offers a 360-degree view of the city and its lagoon. Given its popularity among tourists and locals alike, the chances of having to queue in order to access it are high, but you can book your time slot online or on the spot.

217 **SKYLINE ROOFTOP BAR**

AT: HILTON MOLINO STUCKY VENICE
Fondamenta San Biagio 810
Giudecca ⑥
+39 041 272 3311
hilton.com

The elegant Skyline Rooftop Bar of this prestigious hotel is open to the public and is one of the best experiences you could have in the city, so you shouldn't miss it: treat yourself to an aperitif with a breathtaking view of Punta della Dogana and the lagoon, with smooth jazz playing in the background. Simply fabulous.

218 PONTE DI QUINTAVALLE

RIGHT AFTER FONDAMENTA SANT'ANNA
Castello ⑤

Venice has more to offer than churches and palaces, and the most suggestive views are not necessarily only from higher ground. This bridge connecting San Pietro di Castello to the less touristy part of the city offers a different view of shipyards and boat-dotted shores. In the distance: the solemn bell tower of St Peter's Basilica.

219 SCALA CONTARINI DEL BOVOLO

Corte Contarini del Bovolo 4303
San Marco ①
+39 041 309 6605
scalacontarini delbovolo.com
gioiellinascostidi venezia.it

One of Venice's most beautiful architectural gems! This spiral staircase combines the two most characteristic and pervasive styles of the city, namely the Renaissance and the Gothic. The most thrilling thing, however, is the sweeping lagoon view from the top of the tower. This site is managed by the Fondazione Venezia, which also takes care of other little-known properties in Venice and organises events and guided tours. Check their website for updates.

220 SAN MARCO CLOCK TOWER

Piazza San Marco
San Marco ①
+39 041 240 5211
torreorologio. visitmuve.it

This iconic landmark of Piazza San Marco offers breathtaking views that stretch across the entire basin, while towering over Via Merceria. As you make the trek up the spiral staircase, you can also take a closer look at the mechanisms of the big clock. Beware: children must be at least 6 years of age to enter.

5 MYSTERIOUS PLACES
to visit at night

221 **PIAZZA SAN MARCO**
San Marco ①

It's not as obvious as it may sound. Come after midnight, position yourself in the middle of the square. While keeping an eye on the lagoon, or on the dark outline of the bell tower, slowly turn in a circle, until all the beauty that surrounds you has gotten under your skin.

222 **PUNTA DELLA DOGANA**
Dorsoduro ②

Sit down at Punta della Dogana, with your legs dangling over the black water, and watch this vast dark body breath beneath your feet... An inspiring experience that taps into the true essence of Venice.

223 **BURANO**
Burano ⑨

Burano and most of the major islands that are overrun by tourists in daytime are completely transformed at night. The size of the island and the complete silence mean you can hear the rippling waves wherever you are. Take a stroll down Fondamenta dei Squeri up to the long wooden bridge, that connects Burano with Mazzorbo and stop to look at the sea, which, at night, is surprisingly tranquil and a splendid sight for sore eyes.

224 FONDAMENTA MISERICORDIA

Cannaregio ④

A stroll down this *fondamenta* strikes the perfect balance between the vitality of the tiny bars that are scattered along the way and the tranquillity of the less crowded areas. Charming glimpses abound, especially at night. If you keep walking westward, you will reach the Ghetto where, especially on Saturday night, you may come across some outdoor celebrations.

225 FONDAMENTA DELL'ARSENALE

Castello ⑤

At night, the Fondamenta dell'Arsenale is immersed in semi-darkness and wrapped in complete silence. Walk to the Padiglione delle Navi (Maritime Museum), cross the bridge and the mighty statue of the Piraeus Lion, which is dramatically lit from below, will be there to welcome you.

225 FONDAMENTA DELL'ARSENALE

5 of the most beautiful **BRIDGES** *in the city*

226 PONTO DE BORGOLOCO

Calle de Borgoloco 5866
Castello ⑤

The curious detail of this bridge is hidden in the iron railing. If you look at it from above, you'll be able to spot a W, and, immediately underneath it, a V, the number 3, and an E. Some people think it refers to King Victor Emmanuel III, and was added under Austrian rule, when some things could not be discussed openly.

227 PONTE DEI SOSPIRI / BRIDGE OF SIGHS

Piazza San Marco
San Marco ①

This bridge is the repository of four centuries of convicts' stories. The bridge, which connected the Doge's palace to the prisons, derives its name from the fact that the convicts who crossed it were often destined never to see the light of day again and sighed as they saw the beauty of Venice one last time.

228 PONTE DELLA COSTITUZIONE

Santa Croce ③

Venice's most modern bridge has a slender profile and a sleek and elegant design. The locals don't particularly care for this work by the Spanish architect Santiago Calatrava. They have complained so much about the glass steps, which they find difficult to navigate, that they will now be replaced with solid stone slabs.

229 PONTE DELL'ARSENALE

Fondamenta dell'Arsenale
Castello ⑤

The Ponte dell'Arsenale was built in the 1930s. You can immediately recognise it because of its pointed profile, which was designed by the engineer Eugenio Miozzi, who was inspired by an ancient drawbridge that was featured in many of Tintoretto's paintings.

230 PONTE POSTE VECIE

Fondamenta delle Beccarie 1608
San Polo ③

This small, blackened wooden bridge is said to be the oldest in Venice, and the Rialto area, where it's located, was one of the first areas to be settled. If you cross it, you'll reach the Antica Trattoria Poste Vecie, a restaurant housed in an old post office.

226 **PONTO DE BORGOLOCO**

5
ROMANTIC CORNERS
for a first kiss

231 **CAMPO ERBERIA**
San Polo ③

This is the area immediately before the Rialto Bridge, on the market side. Despite its central location, it's a little secluded from the chaos of the main street. What could be more romantic than meeting up here for a date, sipping a glass of wine, and watching the water buses glide along the Canal Grande?

232 **GIUDECCA**
Giudecca ⑥

If you want to impress your date, then go for a walk along the Fondamenta San Biagio, which is quite spacious and lined with trees. Then wrap up the afternoon at the Skyline Rooftop Bar, which offers stunning views of the whole city. A sure-fire hit.

233 **THE VENICE GIARDINI**
BEHIND THE BRITISH PAVILION
Castello ⑤

Seek out this well-hidden bar in the Biennale gardens, behind the British pavilion. From the tables, among the greenery, you can see the lagoon and the bell tower of San Giorgio. A truly enchanting perspective.

234 CORTE DELLA COMARE

Dorsoduro ②

Venice has plenty of small romantic squares. But this one is particularly charming and quiet, and therefore often frequented by couples. Corte della Comare is a small stretch among narrow houses, featuring an arch and crowned in ivy, and open to the *rio*. Really romantic.

235 GARDEN OF PALAZZO SORANZO CAPPELLO

Ramo Quinto Gallion o del Pezzetto 770
Santa Croce ③

The offices of the art superintendence are housed in the building across the garden, so you can visit it during working hours. This leafy space is a feast of columns, Roman statues and fruit trees, but there is also a wilder section that resembles a delightful romantic garden.

234 CORTE DELLA COMARE

5

CAMPI *(squares) where* VENETIANS HANG OUT

236 **CAMPO SANTA MARGHERITA**
Dorsoduro ②

The heart of university life in Venice, this *campo* comes alive during aperitif time. This is the perfect meeting place for an *ombra* and a chat, where people like to linger until late at night.

236 CAMPO SANTA MARGHERITA

237 CAMPO SAN GIACOMO DELL'ORIO

San Polo ③

In the summer, it's customary for Venetians to roam from one square to another, especially when it comes to participating in festivals and celebrations. The one held in Campo San Giacomo dell'Orio is particularly popular with long communal tables, concerts every night, song and dance. All the festive atmosphere of a village fair.

238 CAMPO SAN POLO

San Polo ③

Campo San Polo is the largest open space after Piazza San Marco. It was considered a popular square, where events and celebrations would take place. Today it's much loved and frequented by Venetians and it's not rare to see children play on the *masegni* (stone floor). In winter, an ice rink is installed here.

239 CAMPO SAN BARNABA

Dorsoduro ②

A small canal that flows placidly to one side, small bars with tables outside on the other, all under the solemn façade of San Barnaba Church. This explains why Campo San Barnaba is so popular with Venetians and students.

240 CAMPO SANT'AGNESE

Dorsoduro ②

Children playing, old ladies chatting, and young people kissing: you'll find the whole inventory of the most authentic Venice in this beautiful *campo,* shaded by large trees and away from the most touristy areas.

5 things to do WHEN IT RAINS

241 **VISIT 'A SQUERO'**

The *squero* (shipyard) is the place where boats are built and maintained. Among the ancient shipyards that have survived in the city to this day is the one in San Trovaso. There is no real visiting time: if it happens to open, you can take a peek inside the workshop by just leaving a small donation.

242 **TAKE A WORKSHOP**

There's something to do for everyone: for instance, you could decorate a mask (*camacana.com*) or take a pottery class (*bochaleri.it*) – both also suitable for children – or you could immerse yourself in the world of silk-screen printing (*fallanivenezia.com*). If crafts are not your cup of tea, there's no shortage of local cooking lessons.

243 **GO TO THE CASINO**

The Casino di Venezia first opened its doors in 1638 in the splendid Renaissance-period Vendramin Calergi palace, a good enough reason in itself for a visit. Please note that you must be at least 18 to enter and that appropriate dress is required.

244 HOP ON A WATER BUS

The water bus (*vaporetto*) number 1 connects Piazzale Roma with the Lido, by way of the Canal Grande, and stops at the most beautiful palaces in Venice. Pick a seat by the window, enjoy the city's perspective from the water and... allow yourself to dream.

245 TAKE A WALK IN THE RAIN

By definition Venice is a city on the water. When it's cloaked in a light fog, and droplets fall into the canals, silencing its deafening noise (even if only for a few minutes), that's perhaps the time when Venice is most true to itself. Do not miss it.

244 HOP ON A WATER BUS

5 *less frequented* FONDAMENTA *for a walk*

246 **FONDAMENTA TOLENTINI**
Santa Croce ③

Fondamenta Tolentini is off the tourist trail. If you go there around dinner time, you'll see plenty of lights and tables here. Head for the Bacareto da Lele, where you can share a glass of white wine with Venetian students. If you like to go out late, you'll find that Campo dei Tolentini is completely deserted at night. Only the Church of San Nicola da Tolentito stands out in the dark, in all its solemn glory.

247 **FONDAMENTA DE LA TANA**
Castello ⑤

This quiet *fondamenta*, near Via Garibaldi, in Castello runs along one of the Biennale venues. Coming from Calle Loredana, you'll stumble upon a curious detail on the left: a plaque on the wall, dating to the Most Serene Republic, which lists the minimum measurements for fish, in order for it to be marketable.

248 FONDAMENTA SANT'EUFEMIA

Giudecca ⑥

The *fondamenta* overlooking the Giudecca canal is all you could wish for if you're eager to go on a quiet walk: a splendid panorama and almost no tourists around. If you arrive by water bus at the Giudecca stop, you may want to have a snack at La Palanca and then head straight to the Church of the Redentore.

249 FONDAMENTA OGNISANTI

Dorsoduro ②

If you find yourself in Fondamenta Zattere ai Ponte Lungo and you want to escape the chaos around you, then turn into Calle Trevisan where you'll find an excellent alternative, Fondamenta Ognisanti, which culminates in a square with a church. The 16th-century building is splendidly decorated with frescoes.

250 FONDAMENTA GASPARO CONTARINI

Cannaregio ④

This is one of the beautiful aspects of Venice: chaotic and incredibly crowded areas alternate with places where you can enjoy a more solitary stroll, where you will rarely come across other people. Fondamenta Gasparo Contarini is an example of this – an area very close to the busy train station, yet isolated and immersed in tranquillity.

5 *fun facts about*
BASILICA SAN MARCO

Piazza San Marco 328
San Marco ①
+39 041 270 8311
basilicasanmarco.it

251 ICON OF THE VIRGIN NICOPEIA

According to legend, this 9th-century, Byzantine-style icon was painted by Saint Luke. You'll find it in the chapel of the same name in the left transept. It has all the elements that are so typical of this period in art: a golden background, a hieratic character, and the centrally positioned subject. The Venetians are particularly devoted to it, particularly because of its legendary provenance.

252 PILLARS OF ACRI

In front of the Basilica's southern façade stand two pillars that were probably brought to Venice as war booty from the portal of the Church of San Saba in Acri. The monoliths are decorated with Egyptian-Syrian monograms, and even today the translation is not entirely clear.

253 STONE ON WHICH ST JOHN THE BAPTIST WAS ALLEGEDLY BEHEADED

For a long time, San Marco's baptistery was home to the stone on which, according to legend, St John the Baptist was beheaded. The saint's blood, which can still be seen on the stone, is said to prove this. For this reason, the monolith is kept in the depot nowadays.

254 THE HEART-SHAPED STONE

If you pay close attention, you'll see a heart-shaped stone with a doge's horn and a hedgehog inside near the Pala d'Oro (Golden Pall). The stone indicates the exact point where the heart of Doge Francesco Erizzo may be buried. The presence of the hedgehog (*riccio*) hints to the doge's last name (Erizzo), to which it was associated by assonance.

255 BAS-RELIEF OF PIETRO ARETINO

On the frame of the door leading from the basilica into the sacristy, you'll come across a number of effigies and bas-reliefs. Oddly enough, you may recognise Pietro Aretino, a decidedly anticlerical Tuscan poet and satirist from the 16th century, who is also portrayed here.

5

GARDENS

to stop and catch your breath

256 GARDEN OF SAN FRANCESCO DELLA VIGNA CHURCH

Ramo Al Ponte San Francesco
Castello ⑤

The complex of San Francesco della Vigna includes a convent, a church, and, above all, a vegetable garden and a vineyard, from which it derives its name. Each of them is extraordinary in itself, but visiting a vineyard in Venice is always a special experience. However, it's not always open to the public, so ask the friars if you can take a guided walk.

256 GARDEN OF SAN FRANCESCO DELLA VIGNA CHURCH

257 GARDEN OF CA' MOROSINI DEL GIARDIN

Calle Val-
marana 4629/B
Cannaregio ④

This garden is located just a few steps from Strada Nova, yet few people know of it. It's nestled within a convent of Dominican nuns, and you must ask permission to visit it. You'll find a vegetable garden with fruit trees, pergolas of white wisteria, roses, and Virginia creeper.

258 PARCO VILLA GROGGIA

Calle del
Capitelo 3160/A
Cannaregio ④

Leafy trees, red benches, children playing, a wellhead, silence, a delightful breeze and the salty air from the lagoon, and even romantic ruins: these are the ingredients of the charming Villa Groggia garden, which is very popular with the locals but mostly unknown to tourists.

259 LAGUNA FIORITA

Fondamenta
Abazia 3546
Cannaregio ④
+39 041 524 4097
lagunafiorita.it

It's the only tree nursery in the historic centre. Go on a stroll through the greenhouses while taking in the nearby Scuola della Misericordia complex. All activities and sales are managed by the Laguna Fiorita Social Co-op, which also works with people with disabilities.

260 GARDEN OF THE REDENTORE CONVENT

Calle dei Frati 194
Giudecca ⑥
+39 041 522 4348

The Redentore Church is linked to a large monastic complex where Capuchin friars still live today. They carry out various activities, including the maintenance of the ancient vegetable garden, with olive trees, vegetables, vines and medicinal herbs that were once used in the adjacent pharmacy, which is still in operation. A peaceful place overlooking the southern lagoon. Visits only by appointment.

5
HAUNTED PALACES
(according to legend)

261 **CA' DARIO**
Campiello
Barbaro 352
Dorsoduro ②

This beautiful building overlooking the Canal Grande is said to be cursed with a terrible spell: it seems as though all those who purchase it will perish by suicide or violent death. This reputation started in the 19th century, when a series of misfortunes befell all the different people who owned the house.

262 **CA' MASTELLI O DEL CAMMELLO**
Calle Tintoretto 3401
Cannaregio ④

Legend has it that this palace is haunted by good-natured ghosts who are none other than its former owners, four merchant brothers, who were turned into stone as a punishment. In fact, you'll recognise them in the four statues that adorn the corners of the nearby Campo dei Mori.

263 **CASINO OF THE SPIRITS**
Fondamenta
Gasparo
Contarini 3541
Cannaregio ④

A haunted house par excellence, Palazzo Contarini dal Zaffo, known as the Casino of the Spirits, owes its fame to a 16th-century legend. An unlucky painter fell in love with one of Giorgione's lovers, but killed himself because of unrequited love. Since then his spirit lingers desperately in this building.

264 MONUMENT TO GIUSEPPE GARIBALDI

Viale Giuseppe Garibaldi
Castello ⑤

Apparently, in 1921 there were several episodes in which a ghost, wearing a red shirt, prevented people from approaching the monument dedicated to Garibaldi at night. The spirit was identified as Giuseppe Zolli, one of the thousands who had sworn to protect his leader forever. This is the origin of the statue erected behind the monument to Garibaldi.

265 JEWISH GHETTO

Cannaregio ④

The presence of a ghost that looked like a 16th-century rabbi in the Italian synagogue was reported for the first time in the 1950s. According to some, the ghost could be the transfiguration of Leone da Modena, a famous figure of Jewish culture.

264 MONUMENT TO GIUSEPPE GARIBALDI

267 BIBLIOTECA DELL'ASSOCIAZIONE SCIENTIFICA PALAZZO CAPPELLO

5 *historic*
LIBRARIES

266 **BIBLIOTECA MONUMENTALE**
AT: SEMINARIO PATRIARCALE DI VENEZIA
Fondamenta Salute 1
Dorsoduro ②
+39 041 274 3973
seminariovenezia.it

This splendid library is located inside the patriarchal seminary and can be visited by appointment. It contains a substantial number of mostly religious texts, the majority of which are at least two centuries old.

267 **BIBLIOTECA DELL'ASSOCIAZIONE SCIENTIFICA PALAZZO CAPPELLO**
Fondamenta Laterano 6391
Castello ⑤
+39 041 522 1307

Palazzo Capello is home to several associations including the Scientific Association of Palazzo Capello and the Centro Internazionale per la Decorazione e il Restauro degli Apparati Decorativi Barocchi e Neoclassici, which boasts a remarkable library of about 10.000 texts on the subject. Even the hall where the volumes are kept is worth visiting for its 16th-century ceiling, terrazzo floor, and decorated exposed beams.

268 LUIGI NONO ARCHIVE

Calle Cosmo 619/621
Giudecca ⑥
+39 041 520 9713
luiginono.it

Luigi Nono was a composer and politician in 20th-century Venice. The foundation named after him was started by Nuria Schönberg Nono and works to preserve and pass down the materials he inherited, such as manuscripts, tapes, books, scores, vinyl, photographs, posters, reviews, and much more.

269 BIBLIOTECA OF SAN LAZZARO DEGLI ARMENI ISLAND

Isola di San Lazzaro degli Armeni ⑧
+39 041 526 0104

The library of the island of San Lazzaro degli Armeni preserves a treasure of an estimated 170.000 volumes, including ancient manuscripts for the most part. The singular hall where they are kept has a controlled atmosphere and a circular shape. Because of a particular acoustic effect, if you stand in the centre of the hall and speak out, you will hear the echo of your own words.

270 ISTITUTO VENETO DI SCIENZE, LETTERE ED ARTI

Campo San Stefano 2945
San Marco ①
+39 041 240 7711
istitutoveneto.it

This prestigious Venetian institute was previously situatued in the Doge's Palace. Today its main office is in Palazzo Loredan, with others spread across various historic buildings in Venice. It preserves 300.000 volumes, which you can access through the national library system, including 17th- and 18th-century editions.

5
CLOISTERS
where you can stop and meditate

271 **DIOCESAN MUSEUM OF VENICE**
AT: CHIOSTRO DI SANT'APOLLONIA
Sestiere Castello 4312
Castello ⑤
+39 041 522 9166
veneziaupt.org

What makes the cloister of St Apollonia, within the diocesan museum, particularly special is that this is the oldest remaining example of a Romanesque court in Venice. Today it's an integral part of the museum itinerary, with Roman and Byzantine stone fragments, mostly from Basilica di San Marco.

272 **CHURCH OF THE MADONNA DELL'ORTO**
Fondamenta Madonna dell' Orto 3512
Cannaregio ④
+39 041 795 991
madonnadellorto.org

Not only is the Church of Madonna dell'Orto a real museum of religious art (several altarpieces by Tintoretto, to begin with), but the adjacent cloister is a lovely peaceful space, with a well and porticoes on three sides. Nowadays it hosts contemporary art exhibitions.

273 CLOISTER OF THE SANTO STEFANO CONVENT

Campo Santo Stefano
San Marco ①

You will find the majestic Gothic Church of St Stephen in Campo Santo Stefano. Once inside, make for the door in the aisle on the left, which leads to the frescoed cloister of the former Augustinian Eremite convent, which was abolished in the 19th century. Today only some fragments of paintings depicting scenes from the Old Testament remain.

274 THE CYPRESS CLOISTER

AT: FONDAZIONE GIORGIO CINI

Isola di San Giorgio Maggiore ⑥
+39 041 271 0211
cini.it

The cypress cloister is an elegant green space inside the Cini Foundation complex, and enclosed, on all sides, by airy renaissance porticos. At the centre, near the well, four magnificent cypress trees rise up, arranged in a symmetrical and elegant order, lending their name to the cloister.

275 DON ORIONE ARTIGIANELLI CULTURAL CENTRE

Rio Terà Foscarini 909/A
Dorsoduro ②
+39 041 522 4077
donorione-venezia.it

This vast complex, covering an area of 10.000 square metres, has four cloisters within its walls, one of which dates back to the 15th century. Today the centre's spaces are mainly used as accommodation and for cultural purposes. As the Biennale and other institutions often include this venue in their calendar of events, you'll be able to visit it more often than not.

5 *charming*
ABANDONED PLACES

276 FORTE SANT'ANDREA

Isola di Sant'Andrea ⑧
+39 0444 193 2124
iluoghidellabbandono.com

How many abandoned 16th-century buildings do you know? Venice is also this: a fortress built to protect the lagoon, an excellent example of military architecture, which today is relegated in a state of semi-ruin, and, perhaps also for this reason, even more charming.

277 COLONIA CA' ROMAN

Pellestrina ⑩
+39 0444 193 2124
iluoghidellabbandono.com

The Ca' Roman summer house was built in the 1930s at the behest of doctor Alberto Graziani. Hundreds of children spent time here, on the beaches of the lagoon. Today it's in a state of complete abandon, but it still retains its appeal. Periodically, photo tours are organised of the premises. Check the website for more info.

278 FORMER HOSPITAL IN POVEGLIA

Isola di Poveglia ⑧
+39 0444 193 2124
iluoghidell abbandono.com

If you are a fan of ghost stories, Poveglia is just up your street. A quarantine zone during the plagues under the Most Serene Republic, it was transformed into a psychiatric hospital in 1924, and closed after World War II. Since then, stories of paranormal activity abound, and even today many people visit it for this precise reason.

279 FORMER HOSPITAL OF SANTA MARIA DELLE GRAZIE

Isola Santa Maria delle Grazie ⑥

The island, also called *La Grazia*, was one of the so-called 'islands of pain', together with San Clemente, San Servolo and Sacca Sessola, and home to hospitals and mental asylums during the last century. The structure was built in the 20th century. Nowadays it's abandoned but arrangements have been made to build apartments and hotels here.

280 OSSUARY OF SANT'ARIANO

Isola Sant'Ariano ⑨

This small, deserted island was settled by different people and in different eras. In 1160, Benedictine nuns founded the monastery of Sant'Adriano here. Today only its foundation and an ossuary, which dates from 1556, remain. You can still catch a glimpse of it despite the perimeter wall.

276 **FORTE SANT'ANDREA**

5
EVENTS
not to be missed

281 **REGATA STORICA**

This regatta is a very important event for the Venetians. It's held the first Sunday of September on the Canal Grande and consists of two parts: the historic parade – a spectacular procession with dozens of old-fashioned boats with rowers wearing period costumes – followed by the proper regatta races.

282 **REGATA DELLE BEFANA**

In the Italian tradition, the *Befana* is an old woman who delivers sweets and gifts to children on the eve of Epiphany. Held on January 6th, this regatta starts from Palazzo Balbi and ends in Rialto. The event is organised by the oldest rowing company in Venice, the Bucintoro. The boats are led by rowers (all men) disguised as Santa Claus and Befanas.

283 SPOSALIZIO DEL MARE

The 'marriage of the sea' ceremony is held on Ascension Day, and consists of a procession of boats, led by the historic boat, called a *bissona,* that carries the mayor of the city to the Church of San Nicolò del Lido, where he throws the ring – blessed by the patriarch of Venice – into the water.

284 REDENTORE

The Feast of the Redeemer is celebrated on the third Sunday of July. It commemorates the liberation of the city from the plague and centres around the votive church on Giudecca. The event ends with a phantasmagorical fireworks display, which the Venetians love to enjoy from their boats moored in San Marco's basin.

285 CARNEVALE

The carnival of Venice is one of the most famous and beloved in the world. It belongs to a centuries-old tradition and is made up of dozens of events, including the Flight of the Angel and the Feast of the Marie. But if you are not a fan of chaos, avoid the most crowded dates: Fat Thursday and Mardi Gras.

5 *tips for* **GONDOLA** *and* **VOGA VENETA** *lovers*

286 **CANOTTIERI GIUDECCA.COM**

The Associazione di Canottieri Giudecca offers courses in traditional Venetian and classic rowing, as well as sailing tours in the lagoon. It also has a women-only group, and you can follow their activities on the blog: *unpodidonne.wordpress.com*

287 **IL FORCOLAIO MATTO**
Ramo dell'Oca 4231
Cannaregio ④
+39 041 877 8823
ilforcolaiomatto.it

The *forcola* is the distinctive oarlock on the boats that are used to navigate Venice's lagoon. It is carved from a single piece of wood, seamlessly combining creativity with functionality. The 'remer' who makes these *forcole* must therefore be a skilled craftsman, just like Piero Dri. Visit his workshop to find out for yourself.

288 ROWVENICE.ORG

Row Venice is an association comprised mainly of women who, in addition to the classic Venetian-style rowing courses, also cater to tourists by offering attractive alternatives such as the *Cicchetto Row*, which includes wine tasting and *cicchetti* during the lesson.

289 LIBRERIA MARE DI CARTA

Fondamenta dei Tolentini 222
Santa Croce ③
+39 041 716 304
maredicarta.com

As its name wisely suggests (Sea of Paper), this is the place for you if you have a keen interest in all things navigation. This shop sells books on the water creatures of Venice, as well as kits to build a miniature gondola, photographic collections of the lagoon and nautical maps to prepare your trip around the world.

290 VENICEONBOARD.IT

On this clear and well-structured website, you'll be able to book various rowing activities, which you can do with friends and family. The offer ranges from lessons in Venetian-style rowing to traditional sailing.

RANDE
GRANDE
RIAPERTURA DEL
MORION
2018/19
MORION

65 PLACES TO ENJOY CULTURE

5 *foundations for* CONTEMPORARY ART *lovers*

291 **ARTISTI ARTIGIANI DEL CHIOSTRO**
AT: FORMER SANTI COSMA E DAMIANO CONVENT
Campo San Cosmo 620
Giudecca ⑥
+39 349 395 2052
artistiartigianidel chiostro.com

Wandering around the cloister of this former convent can be an inspiring experience. The whole complex underwent a massive restoration, during which workshops and studios for young artists were built. Here art is made rather than displayed.

291 ARTISTI ARTIGIANI DEL CHIOSTRO

5
THEATRES
not to miss

311 **TEATRO LA FENICE**
Campo San Fantin 1965
San Marco ①
+39 041 786 654
teatrolafenice.it

La Fenice is THE theatre of Venice. Do try to get tickets to see an opera here: you'll be rewarded with one the most exciting experiences that you could possibly have in Venice. Despite its rococo appearance, the inner hall was completely rebuilt after a fire devastated the opera in 1996. A phoenix always rises from its ashes.

312 **TEATRO MALIBRAN**
Campiello del Teatro 5873
Cannaregio ④⑤
+39 041 965 1975
teatrolafenice.it

The theatre dates back to the second half of the 17th century. Heavily remodelled over the centuries, it reopened in its current form in 2001, after an important restoration. Both here, and at La Fenice, they schedule a good programme of operas and chamber music as well as concerts of the Fenice Philharmonic Orchestra.

313 TEATRO GOLDONI

Calle del Teatro 4650/B San Marco ①
+39 041 240 2011
teatrostabileveneto.it

This theatre is the go-to place for prose in Venice, as its name suggests. Carlo Goldoni (1707 – 1793) is the city's most famous playwright. They always perform some of his comedies here during the season. The programme also includes concerts and contemporary drama.

314 TEATRO AL'AVOGARIA

Corte Zappa 1617 Dorsoduro ②
+39 041 099 1967
teatro-avogaria.it

The theatre was founded at the beginning of the last century, as part of a school of thought that promoted the renewal of the arts. Today it hosts an acting school and a series of festivals that cover all aspects of contemporary theatre.

315 TEATRO PICCOLO ARSENALE

Campiello Tana 2169/F Castello ⑤
+39 041 521 8711
labiennale.org

The Piccolo is housed in a sprawling 16th-century warehouse space within the Arsenale. By altering the historic building, the architect was able to create an evocative space, equipped with advanced stage technology. It hosts many dance, theatre, and music events linked to the Biennale's schedule.

5 churches with TINTORETTO masterpieces

316 **CHURCH OF SANTA MARIA MATER DOMINI**
Corte Piossi 2116
Santa Croce ③

This simple renaissance church stands on the site of a previous building dedicated to Saint Christina. Today it has a Greek cross plan, with three naves. In the left branch of the transept hangs a work by Tintoretto from 1561, titled *The Invention of the Cross*.

317 **CHURCH OF SAN TROVASO**
Fondamenta Bonlini 380
Dorsoduro ②

The Church of Saints Gervasius and Protasius, called San Trovaso, has a very long history, which is linked to the founding of Venice. In the chapel of the Sacrament, on the left side of the transept, you can see a copy of Jacopo Tintoretto's painting of *The Last Supper* as well as a copy of *Christ Washing the Disciples' Feet*. The original is at the National Gallery in London.

318 CHURCH OF SAN CASSIANO

Calle dei Morti
Santa Croce ③

The Church of San Cassiano probably dates back to the 10th century, although the interior is richly decorated with baroque stuccoes and marble and paintings from different eras. The main altar features some works by Tintoretto including the altarpiece depicting *The Resurrection of Christ* with Saint Cassiano and Saint Cecilia, *The Descent Into Limbo,* and *The Crucifixion.*

319 CHURCH OF SAN POLO

Campo San Polo
San Polo ③
+39 041 275 0462
chorusvenezia.org

The Church of San Polo, which is located in one of the largest and most popular squares, probably dates back to the 9th century, even though it underwent major restorations in the 16th century. As a result, you can see works here today by the likes of Tintoretto (*Last Supper*) and Veronese (*Marriage of the Virgin*) as well as ceiling painting in the sacristy by Giandomenico Tiepolo.

320 CHURCH OF SAINT ROCH

Campo San Rocco 3063
San Polo ③

The Church of Saint Roch is linked to the story of the nearby Scuola Grande. The interior is richly decorated with frescoes and paintings. The imposing narrative work by Tintoretto, whose paintings depict the last events of the life of the Saint, is especially worth looking out for.

5 *alternative*
EXPOSITION SPACES

321 SPAZIO PUNCH
Fondamenta San Biagio 800/O
Giudecca ⑥
+39 348 890 9065
spaziopunch.com

It's not easy to define this chameleon-like place that changes skin with every event. Suffice it to say that it's a reclaimed former industrial structure, which has been stripped down to the bone. Each new artistic project is set up with special conceptual arrangements, be it a Biennale-related event or an independent exhibition.

322 LABORATORIO OCCUPATO MORION
Calle del Morion 2951
Castello ⑤
+39 041 528 8519

This space, which is situated in a working-class area, far removed from tourist and commercial routes, has been occupied since 1990. When they are not mounting political protests or demonstrating against cruise ships, they organise exhibitions, cultural events, and grandiose parties.

321 SPAZIO PUNCH

323 **M9 – MUSEO DEL '900**

Via Giovanni Pascoli 11
Mestre ⑩
+39 041 099 5941
m9museum.it

A good example of a new-style museum without a permanent collection of dusty, historic objects. Instead you are treated to engaging installations using state of the art technology – VR glasses, holograms and interactive projections – to narrate the compelling history of the 20th century and its many changes and evolutions in a dynamic way. Highly recommended, even for very young visitors.

324 **GAD – GIUDECCA ART DISTRICT**

Fondamenta San Giacomo 211/B
Giudecca ⑥
giudecca-art-district.com

GAD, a network of contemporary art projects and professionals, was founded in 2019 and is based in the many fascinating industrial spaces on the island of Giudecca. The association aims to develop an ongoing programme of exhibitions, residencies and artist studios. Each year, GAD will propose a theme and a curatorial approach, which will serve as a leitmotif for artistic-cultural projects that are open to all.

325 **CREATURE DI GOMMA - VENICE VINTAGE TOY**

Calle de la Vida 2390/A
San Polo ③
+39 347 428 7621
creaturedigomma.com

This quirky museum is home to over 5000 rubber toys. Most of the specimens were produced between the 1950s and the 1980s and they are all linked to the world of animated cartoons and comics. Older visitors will enjoy this trip down nostalgia lane, and the opportunity to show their childhood heroes to their children.

5 wonderful MOSAICS in Basilica di San Marco

326 **THE MOSAIC OF THE DODECAHEDRON**
Piazza San Marco 328
San Marco ①
+39 041 270 8311
basilicasanmarco.it

The dodecahedron had many interpretations in classical antiquity. For Plato, it was the symbol of harmony in nature; but it was also associated with Venus, the planet of Venice. This is what probably inspired Paolo Uccello to recreate it in the magnificent mosaic of the atrium, by the main doorway.

326 THE MOSAIC OF THE DODECAHEDRON

327 THE RHINOCEROS MOSAIC

Inside, on the left-hand side of the basilica, in front of the Chapel of St Isidore, there is an unusual representation of a rhinoceros with a stylised red tree in the background. The dating, meaning and symbology are uncertain, but some see a link with 'power', or interpret it as a talisman against disease.

328 LOZENGE OF RED PORPHYRY

A lozenge of red porphyry has been inlaid in the floor of the Basilica vestibule, in front of the main entrance. It marks the exact spot where emperor Federico Barbarossa would have knelt before Pope Alexander III in 1177.

329 THE MOSAIC OF THE CHRIST PANTOCRATOR

All the mosaics of the basilica do not date from the same period. On the contrary even, they were produced over a long period of time, probably following a rigorous iconographic programme. The oldest mosaic? The one in the apse, representing Christ Pantocrator, which was heavily reworked in the 16th century.

330 THE MOSAIC OF THE TWO COCKS

Finding all the animals that are portrayed inside the basilica is a game that may take some time. Start with the pavement near the altar of the Madonna Nicopeia, where you can distinguish two cocks who are carrying a trussed-up fox. These symbols probably refer to the virtues and vices that were attributed to animals in the Middle Ages.

5 places to visit if you love SHAKESPEARE

331 **IL BANCO ROSSO**
Calle Ghetto Vecchio 2912
Cannaregio ④
+39 041 740 317
bancorosso.org

The oldest pawnshop in the Jewish ghetto is now open to the public, and you can also visit the small museum. Supposedly, Shakespeare was inspired by this place when writing his play *The Merchant of Venice*. The name derives from the colour of the receipts that customers received in exchange for their possessions.

332 **THE HOUSE OF OTHELLO**
Campo dei Carmini 2615
Dorsoduro ②

Campo dei Carmini is where Cristoforo Moro lived. He was a Venetian patrician who allegedly inspired Shakespeare to create the figure of Othello. And in fact, there are plenty of similarities: he was a galley captain who lost his wife while he was away in Cyprus for three years. He remarried a woman whose nickname was the 'white demon'.

333 **THE RIALTO BRIDGE**
San Polo ①③

Everyone knows the Rialto Bridge of course. But most people will have no idea that Shakespeare mentioned it in *The Merchant of Venice*. Although we can't be sure that the bard ever visited Italy, he nonetheless seems to know the city well enough.

334 THE HOUSE OF DESDEMONA

AT: PALAZZO CONTARINI FASAN

Campiello Contarina 2307
San Marco ①

If we are to believe that Cristoforo Moro was the flesh and blood version of Othello, then the house of his second wife (nicknamed 'the white demon') could be the residence of Desdemona. We're referring to Palazzo Contarini Fasan of course, a narrow and lavishly-decorated building that overlooks the Canal Grande.

335 THE JEWISH GHETTO

Cannaregio ④

The Jewish ghetto was formerly the area of the foundries, the so-called *getto*, where the metals were cast (*gettare*). The term that we use nowadays derives from an error in the pronunciation of this word. This is also where one of Shakespeare's most famous characters, Shylock the moneylender, lived.

334 THE HOUSE OF DESDEMONA

5
BUILDINGS *to visit (only) during the* BIENNALE

336 **PALAZZO BARBARO**
Campiello Pisani 2840
San Marco ①
+39 349 650 3892
labiennale.org

Two palaces actually make up this complex: Palazzo Barbaro Curtis, which dates back to the 1400s, and its extension, Palazzo Barbaro. The Biennale has been using the ground floor in Palazzo Barbaro since 2015 for side exhibitions. It's worth visiting just for the breathtaking view of the Canal Grande.

337 **PALAZZO BEMBO**
Riva del Carbon 4793-4785
San Marco ①
+39 346 760 3386
palazzobembo.org

Although the interior has been heavily remodelled, the façade of this beautiful palace, which overlooks the Canal Grande, remains quite faithful to the original Venetian Gothic style. Today the building is home to a hotel, but during the Biennale it also hosts side events.

338 CATALONIA IN VENICE

Calle de Quintavale 40/A Castello ⑤

Walking to this place is already an experience in itself but it gives you an opportunity to visit one of the most authentic places in Venice. For many years, the Ramon Llull Institute has been hosting events with a link to Catalonia in this evocative setting, where boats are moored in winter. During the Biennale, this place is awash with light, poetry and art.

339 PALAZZO DONÀ DALLE ROSE

Fondamente Nove 5038 Cannaregio ④ +39 380 154 1468

The historic home of the Donà dalle Rose family was erected in the 17th century at the behest of Doge Leonardo Donà dalle Rose. It has two façades, both in the late renaissance style, one facing the Rio dei Gesuiti, and the main one facing the island of Murano and the northern lagoon.

340 CHURCH OF SANTA CROCE DEGLI ARMENI

Rio Terrà de le Colonne 1059 San Marco ① +39 041 526 0104

Finding this small church is not an easy undertaking. Its modest entrance is hidden in a *sotoportego*. Visiting it may be prove even more difficult however. Nonetheless, this small 12th-century building is an important testimony to the history of the Armenian community and the cosmopolitan and welcoming tradition of Venice.

5 cultural venues with PHOTOGRAPHY *and* ARCHITECTURAL EXHIBITIONS

341 **CASA DEI TRE OCI**
Fondamenta Zitelle 43
Giudecca ⑥
+39 041 241 2332
treoci.org

This gallery is the best in Venice for photo exhibitions. The building has a famous past, like so many other palaces in Venice. Initially it was the mansion of an intellectual, then it became the residence of many artistic personalities. Nowadays it's a museum, with a wonderful view over the Doge's Palace.

342 **WILMOTTE FOUNDATION**
Fondamenta dell'Abazia 3560
Cannaregio ④
+39 041 476 1160
fondationwilmotte.com

This destination is definitely off the beaten path. The building serves as the Venetian headquarters of this French Foundation, which promotes art, architecture, and photography. In spring it's worth the trip even just for the entrance to the palace, which is immersed in oleanders and for the timeless atmosphere of the rooms.

343 **PALAZZO CINI GALLERY**
AT: PALAZZO FOSCARINI
Campo San Vio 864
Dorsoduro ②
+39 041 241 1281
palazzocini.it

The Palazzo Cini Gallery is located inside Palazzo Foscarini and is the legacy of the entrepreneur and politician Vittorio Cini who, in his lifetime, collected a huge number of artworks, which are now exhibited here. It also hosts temporary exhibitions dedicated to photography, architecture, and design.

344 **FONDAZIONE PRADA**
Ca' Corner della Regina 2215
Santa Croce ③
+39 041 810 9161
fondazioneprada.org

Situated inside the splendid 18th-century palazzo of Ca' Corner della Regina, this is the Venetian headquarters of the Prada Foundation. Since 2011, you can admire it in all its splendour and enjoy the cultural initiatives it promotes, which encompass all forms of contemporary art including painting, photography, sculpture, cinema and design.

345 **FONDAZIONE BERENGO**
AT: PALAZZO CAVALLI FRANCHETTI
Campo Santo Stefano 2847
San Marco ①
+39 041 739 453
fondazioneberengo.org

The Berengo foundation has always had a soft spot for Murano and its most precious resource, the artisanal ability to work with glass. But it also promotes contemporary art, architecture and design in an inclusive way. This explosive mix translates into exhibitions and events that are always worth seeing.

5
ART GALLERIES

346 **HOLLY SNAPP GALLERY**
Calle delle Botthege 3133
San Marco ①
+39 041 296 0824
hollysnappgallery.com

While the artist Geoffrey Humphries divides his time between London and Giudecca, where he has his workshop, his wife manages the gallery that sells his works (and those of other artists), including Venetian landscapes, still-lifes and nudes.

347 **GALLERIA MASTINU GIORGIO**
Calle Crosera 3126
San Marco ①
+39 347 182 8553
giorgiomastinufineart.it

This space probably holds the Guinness record for Venice's smallest art gallery. But fear not: the quality is just compressed into a smaller space. Mainly known for its works on paper, such as drawings, photographs, prints, books and more.

348 **CONTINI ART GALLERY**
Calle Larga XXII Marzo 2288
San Marco ①
+39 041 523 0357
continiarte.com

The Contini Art Gallery has been a fixture on Venice's art scene for forty years. Nowadays it occupies an impressive five-storey building where artworks by some of the greatest artists of the past and present are exhibited including Fernando Botero, Julian Schnabel, and Christo, just to name a few.

349 **CATERINA TOGNON ART GALLERY**

Corte Barozzi 2158
San Marco ①
+39 348 856 1818
caterinatognon.com

This major gallery, in Palazzo Treves, exhibits glasswork, collaborating with artists from the Studio Glass movement. It is one of the main European galleries dedicated to this medium.

350 **GALERIE DOROTHEA VAN DER KOELEN**

Calle dei Calegheri 2566
San Marco ①
+39 041 520 7415
galerie.vanderkoelen.de

Dorothea van der Koelen founded her first gallery at just 19 years of age. She now has a total of three, plus two publishing houses and an art magazine. The Italian branch follows a clear and rigorous programme, with a wide range of events.

348 **CONTINI ART GALLERY**

5 stories about the

CAPITALS OF THE DOGE'S PALACE

351 **BIRDS WITH PREY**
AT: PALAZZO DUCALE
Piazza San Marco 1
San Marco ①
+39 041 271 5911
palazzoducale.visitmuve.it

If you pay close attention, you will spot a number of capitals that are engraved with birds and their prey: a stork in the act of eating a snake, a bird devouring a fish, and finally an ibis. According to medieval symbolism, birds are influenced by signs of the solstice and equinox and represent sentient life.

351 BIRDS WITH PREY

352 THE MONTHS OF THE YEAR

The astral and also the Venetian calendars began in March, which was symbolised by a double-horn player. April is represented in the bas-relief of a bull, and May with a rose. June brings cherries, July wheat and so on. Each month is associated with a product of the earth or a zodiac sign.

353 DEADLY SINS

The seven cardinal sins are represented by just as many very vivid allegories: Gluttony eats and drinks greedily, Lust is a woman who uncovers her breasts and gazes at herself in the mirror, Wrath tears off her clothes, and so on. Can you spot them all, and above all, guess which sin is which?

354 CRAFTS

The capitals of the Doge's Palace also depict various crafts, which can be recognised by the different headpieces that were attributed to each profession. You can distinguish the notary, the goldsmith, the blacksmith, the cobbler, and even shop assistants – the only ones that are bareheaded.

355 BIBLICAL EPISODES

The corner capitals are decorated with representations of biblical episodes, arranged to narrate a single story, starting from the southwest capital that depicts the creation of Adam.

LIBRERIA SULLALUNA

25 THINGS TO DO WITH CHILDREN

5 *great* BOOKSHOPS *for children*

356 **LIBRERIA SULLALUNA**
Fondamenta Misericordia 2535
Cannaregio ④
+39 041 722 924
sullalunavenezia.it

An enchanting place to take a break, perfect for the whole family. It's a bar-bookshop-bistro that serves good food and sells a nice selection of graphic novels and comic books, with some real gems for children. They also have a good section on Venice.

357 **EDITIONS DU DROMADAIRE**
Barabaria delle Tole 6656
Castello ⑤
+39 041 529 9014
dromadaire.it

The books of this tiny publishing house are real masterpieces. You'll find Dromalibri, their collection of lovely handbound editions with poetic illustrations, in the workshop in Barbaria delle Tole. The Dromadarte collection comprises limited editions of books that are entirely handmade, as well as the splendid prints of the artists Florence Faval and Pierre Hornain, who came up with the idea of this magnificent publishing project.

358 BIBLIOTECA BETTINI JUNIOR

Campo San Provolo 4704/A
Castello ⑤
+39 041 522 0557
comune.venezia.it

A day at the library? Why not. The Bettini Junior Library not only has volumes specifically for children, but is also a very active centre for events and meetings of all kinds, from comic book workshops to fairy tales set to music, book presentations to rap music and stop-motion workshops.

359 ZAZÀ COMIC SHOP FUMETTERIA

Calle dell'Olio 2424
San Polo ③
+39 041 822 3204
zazacomics. business.site

While a comic book shop is not exclusively a place for children, this small shop is also suitable for those adults who haven't fully grown up yet. The selection of comic books is quite impressive, ranging from classics to fiction, larded with politicsand current affairs.

360 LIBRERIA MARCOPOLO

Campo Santa Margherita 2899
Dorsoduro ②
+39 041 822 4843

Fondamenta Ponte Lungo 282
Giudecca ⑥
+39 041 847 3867
libreriamarcopolo.com

MarcoPolo is an independent bookshop with two locations, one in Dorsoduro, the other on Giudecca. Here you will find elegant titles and illustrated books for adults and children. The children's book section is very well stocked. They also organise meetings with authors and photography courses.

5 *amazing kid-friendly* MUSEUMS

361 **MUSEO STORICO NAVALE / MUSEUM OF NAVAL HISTORY**

Riva San Biasio 2148
Castello ⑤
+39 041 244 1399
marina.difesa.it

See those two impressive anchors marking an entrance. Welcome to the Museum of Naval History where you can learn more about Venice's history as a proud maritime city, through weapons, paintings, and cannons. The must-see? The bucentaur, or *bucintoro,* the glorious golden state barge that carried the Doge during the Ascension Day celebrations.

362 **PADIGLIONE DELLE NAVI / SHIP PAVILION**

Fondamenta Rio della Tana 2126/C
Castello ⑤
+39 041 244 1399
visitmuve.it

After leaving the Naval History Museum, head towards the Fondamenta dell'Arsenale. Just before the bridge of Paradise, you can visit the Ship Pavilion with the same ticket, and see all kinds of Venetian boats.

363 MUSEO DI FISICA ANTONIO MARIA TRAVERSI / PHYSICS MUSEUM

AT: LICEO MARCO FOSCARINI

Fondamenta Santa Caterina 4942
Cannaregio ④
+39 347 863 8987
museo.liceofoscarini.it

The most peculiar aspect of this museum is that it's located in a school. Your tour guides are the pupils themselves. The institution was founded during the Napoleonic era, when the then director, Abbot Antonio Maria Traversi, an important physicist, donated his precious collection of scientific instruments to the school.

364 MUSEO DI STORIA NATURALE / MUSEUM OF NATURAL HISTORY

Salizada del Fontego dei Turchi 1730
Santa Croce ③
+39 041 275 0206
msn.visitmuve.it

This museum, which is housed in the Fondaco dei Turchi, attracts very few visitors strangely enough. The Museum of Natural History is a great place for children and adults alike, offering a well-organised display and a very engaging itinerary, with a section dedicated to the lagoon and, last but not least, dinosaur skeletons.

365 LA BIBLIOTECA DEL COLORE DELLA FORNACE ORSONI / ORSONI'S COLOUR LIBRARY

Calle dei Vedei 1045/A
Cannaregio ④
+39 041 244 0002
orsoni.com

The best bit about the Orsoni glassworks, the only one still in operation in Venice, is the Orsoni's Colour Library, an amazing display of 3000 shades of gold leaf glass. A room where craftsmanship and history are blended with poetry.

5 *great shops*
FOR CHILDREN

366 **PONTE DEI SOGNI**
Salizada San
Antonin 3473
Castello ⑤
+39 041 520 3057

One of the few real toy shops left in the heart of Venice. In this little family-run shop, you can find children's books inspired by Venice and designed by the artist Giorgio Ghidòli, wooden toys from Alto Adige, little trinkets, and board games, all in the *Serenissima* theme.

367 **SIGNOR BLUM**
Campo San
Barnaba 2840
Dorsoduro ②
+39 041 522 6367
signorblum.it

How can you resist the bright window display of Signor Blum, a historic shop and workshop? Here you can shop for puzzles, watches, small Venetian houses, collectibles. Everything here is very colourful and strictly handmade.

368 **AL PUPO**
Strada Nova 2212
Cannaregio ④
+39 041 719 922
alpupo.it

This family-owned shop has dressed many generations of Venetian children. Here you'll find everything you need to dress your child like a little lord, from sumptuous christening dresses, to pretty handmade shoes and all kinds of fun accessories including hats, pinafores and much more. All made in Italy, it goes without saying.

369 BARCHETTA DI CARTA DI MARIA MARIANO

Calle dei Cristi 1731
San Polo ③
+39 041 564 6888
barchettadicarta.wordpress.com

A delightful little shop where the owner – who also restores books and illustrations – makes most of the items on display herself. She sells paper objects for the bedroom and the most adorable stuffed animals, each with its own name and its own story.

370 GILBERTO PENZO

Calle Seconda dei Saoneri 2681
San Polo ③
+39 041 524 6139
veniceboats.com

It's hard to imagine a more authentic Venetian shop than this one. It is the soul of the city… in miniature. The models of all sizes and complexity recreate different historical boats, and are a great way to help children understand the lagoon's fundamentals by playing.

370 GILBERTO PENZO

5

CAMPI

where children can play safely

371 **CORTE DEI CORDAMI**
Calle Corte dei Cordami
Giudecca ⑥

The shape of this unusually long square refers to its history. They used to produce hemp ropes here in the old days. In the summer, you'll often see old women sitting on their doorstep while children chase each other around the wellhead.

371 CORTE DEI CORDAMI

372 **PARCO DELLE RIMEMBRANZE S. ELENA / PARK OF REMEMBRANCE**

Castello ⑤

The St Elena gardens are probably the largest park in Venice, a beautiful green area full of plants and trees in a less touristy area of Venice, where children can play safely. From here you can enjoy breathtaking views of the lagoon and the Lido, especially on summer nights.

373 **GIARDINI REALI / ROYAL GARDENS**

San Marco ①

The Royal Gardens are ideal for taking a break with your little ones. They are conveniently located behind the Marciana National Library. You'll often find groups of students on a field trip and children of all ages enjoying the open space before their next visit.

374 **GIARDINI DI CA' REZZONICO GARDENS**

Fondamenta Rezzonico
Dorsoduro ②

A small and graceful garden in the heart of Venice, a place that offers plenty of peace and quiet with benches and Italian-style hedges. An excellent idea when you need a break from the melée in the museums in the centre.

375 **GIARDINO MARINARESSA GARDENS**

Riva dei Sette Martiri
Castello ⑤

This beautiful tree-lined garden that overlooks the lagoon is influenced (in a positive way!) by the proximity of the historic headquarters of the Biennale. During the art show, the garden hosts many related events, and contemporary art pieces and sculptures are installed here on a rotating basis.

5 *fun* ACTIVITIES *children will love*

376 **CERAMIC CLASS**
AT: I BOCHALERI
Viale Giuseppe
Garibaldi 1257
Castello ⑤
+39 346 591 3578
bochaleri.it

Venice is renowned for its glass, its masks and its lace, but the city also has a longstanding tradition of artisan ceramics, and those who practice this are keen to share it. For this reason, the I Bochaleri association was founded in 2003, with the aim of protecting and making this practice more popular, by organising workshops for adults and children.

377 **ARCHERY**
AT: COMPAGNIA ARCIERI DEL LEON
Via Malamocco 14/B
Lido di Venezia ⑧
+39 041 276 0223
arcierileon.it

Archery club La Compagnia Arcieri del Leon organises courses for beginners, who must be at least nine years old to join. If you're a beginner, there's an eight-hour crash-course, at the end of which you'll receive a certificate. All equipment is provided.

378 **DECORATING A MASK**
AT: CA' MACANA
Calle de le
Boteghe 3172
Dorsoduro ②
+39 041 277 6142
camacana.com

This historic mask shop offers individual and group workshops in Italian, English, and Russian. You can choose your mask and decorate it with 12 different techniques. What better souvenir of Venice than a mask you created with your own hands?

379 SILK-SCREEN PRINTING WORKSHOP

AT: FALLANI VENEZIA-CENTER FOR THE ARTS
Calle del Magazzen 4875
Cannaregio ④
+39 041 523 5772
fallanivenezia.com

This fascinating workshop was founded in 1968, by Fiorenzo Fallani, who imported the art of silkscreen printing from the United States. Today this important art centre collaborates with museums and commercial enterprises. They offer two kinds of activities, for individuals and for families. Check their website for prices and schedules.

380 SCUBA DIVING CLASSES

AT: SPIAGGIA HOTEL EXCELSIOR
Lungomare Guglielmo Marconi
Lido di Venezia ⑧

This scuba diving school offers introductory activities for children who are four and older. The youngest ones will particularly appreciate the snorkelling classes, while children ten and older can participate in real diving sessions.

378 DECORATING A MASK

25 PLACES TO SLEEP

5
CONVENTS
where you can spend the night

381 **ISTITUTO CANOSSIANO SAN TROVASO**
Fondamenta de le Romite 1323/A
Dorsoduro ②
+39 041 240 9711
romite1323.com

The perfect accommodation if you are looking for a simple and clean shelter for the night, the Istituto Canossiano will allow you to fall asleep in absolute silence and tranquillity, and at the same time get around easily during the day, thanks to its central position.

382 **THE SAN GIORGIO ABBEY**
Isola di San Giorgio Maggiore ⑥
+39 041 522 7827
abbaziasangiorgio.it

If you decide to stay in one of the five rooms of the abbey of San Giorgio, you must keep in mind two things: you will sleep in one of the most enchanting places in Venice, famous for its history and art, and your stay will allow you to appreciate and share the life of a community.

383 **CENTRO CULTURALE DON ORIONE ARTIGIANELLI**
Rio Terà Foscarini 909/A
Dorsoduro ②
+39 041 522 4077
donorione-venezia.it

The Don Orione Artigianelli cultural centre is a very large structure and includes spaces for cultural events, exhibitions, and conferences. It houses four different cloisters within its walls and is located in the heart of the Dorsoduro district. The rooms are simple but comfortable and immersed in the most restful silence.

384 DOMUS CILIOTA

Calle delle
Muneghe 2976
San Marco ①
+39 041 520 4888
ciliota.it

This former Augustinian convent is located just a few minutes from Piazza San Marco. It was founded at the end of the 15th century and abolished by Napoleon. The rooms overlook a beautiful cloister garden and certainly are more comfortable than what you'd expect to find in a monastery. Good value for your money.

385 CASA CABURLOTTO

Fondamenta
Rizzi 316
Santa Croce ③
+39 041 710 877
casacaburlotto.it

Located near the train station, this former convent's position is definitely worth considering if you brought a lot of heavy luggage. It's still handy for getting to the centre of the city and offers simple, clean rooms at more than reasonable prices. The icing on the cake: the garden.

383 CENTRO CULTURALE DON ORIONE ARTIGIANELLI

5 lovely
B & Bs by a canal

386 **HOTEL PENSIONE ACCADEMIA-VILLA MARAVEGE**
Fondamenta
Bollani 1058
Dorsoduro ②
+39 041 521 0188
pensioneaccademia.it

In the area behind the Canal Grande, this delightful hotel overlooks an open and airy *rio*, with striking views of the opposite side of the canal. The rooms are furnished in the Venetian style and some of them overlook the pretty garden of the inn.

387 **PENSIONE SEGUSO**
Calle Pisto 779
Dorsoduro ②
+39 041 528 6858
pensioneseguso.com

The splendid Seguso inn has been in business for 100 years. And today, just like at the beginning, it's a wonderful family-run business. The highlight of this accommodation is undoubtedly the view of the Giudecca Canal. Reasonably priced.

388 **GENERATOR**
Fondamenta
Zitelle 86
Giudecca ⑥
+39 041 877 8288
generatorhostels.com

The ideal accommodation for young travellers. This B&B is very well-kept in each and every aspect, and is located on the Giudecca Canal, in the less touristy area of Venice, but still convenient to reach the centre.

389 ANTICA LOCANDA MONTIN

Fondamenta
Borgo 1147
Dorsoduro ②
+39 041 522 7151
locandamontin.com

A historic family-run hotel since the 19th century, the Monti inn has been offering simple but welcoming accommodations. Several celebrities have stayed here in the past. The best part is the restaurant with a beautiful garden where fresh fish is served.

390 B&B CA' FUJIYAMA

Calle Lunga San
Barnaba 2727/A
Dorsoduro ②
+39 041 724 1042
bedandbreakfast-fujiyama.it

A Japanese-style bed & breakfast in the heart of Venice? Why not. The Fujiyama B&B has only four rooms – small but nice and comfortable. Even if you do not stay here, it's worth stopping in the inn's tearoom, which offers absolutely delicious and refined infusions in a small garden adorned with wisteria and jasmine.

388 GENERATOR

5

SMALL HOTELS

for sweet dreams

391 **POLO'S TREASURES**
Calle del
Campaniel 1796
San Polo ③
+39 041 524 3785
polostreasures.it

It's not a proper hotel per se but an old building that was renovated with great care and divided into apartments, furnished in the Venetian style with a contemporary twist. A small and comfortable nest right in the middle of the city.

391 POLO'S TREASURES

392 **PALAZZO SODERINI**

Campo Bandiera e Moro 3611
Castello ⑤
+39 041 296 0823
palazzosoderini.it

A small B&B that is furnished in a basic but tasteful manner, and located in Castello. It's well served by public transportation and not far from Piazza San Marco. In summer, breakfast is served in the small and delightful garden.

393 **OLTRE IL GIARDINO**

Fondamenta Contarini 2542
San Polo ③
+39 041 275 0015
oltreilgiardino-venezia.com

It's rare to find a large house surrounded by a garden in Venice. The composer and author Alma Mahler loved this one so much that she decided to make it her home. Nowadays it's a hotel with refined details and spacious rooms, located in the heart of Venice.

394 **AVOGARIA 5 ROOMS**

Calle dell' Avogaria 1629
Dorsoduro ②
+39 041 296 0491
avogaria.com

Avogaria is a small hotel with only 5 rooms, a well-furnished nook where you will receive a warm welcome. Despite its location in Dorsoduro, in an area that is slightly out of the centre compared to major places of interest, it is well served by water buses.

395 **CASA BURANO**

Fondamenta Santa Caterina 3 (reception)
Isola di Mazzorbo ⑨

Via Giudecca 139 (rooms)
Burano ⑨
+39 041 527 2281
casaburano.it

The rooms of this hotel are dispersed among some of the houses of Burano, located in the most strategic spots on the island. Breakfast is served in pretty picnic baskets, which allow guests to eat outside and enjoy the island before tourists arrive.

5 very EXCLUSIVE hotels

396 **ISOLA SANTA CRISTINA**
Isola Santa Cristina ⑨
+39 041 520 2702
vovcollection.com

You need just three words to define this place: mends the soul. This private island, which can be rented as a whole, is an oasis of peace and silence, among vineyards, orchards, and peacocks. One night here, and whatever your grievance, the sweetness of the place will dissolve it.

397 **HOTEL DANIELI**
Riva degli Schiavoni
Calle Seconda de
la Fava 4196
Castello ⑤
+39 041 522 6480
danielihotelvenice.com

More than a hotel, the Danieli is a legend. It opened in the 19th century and has hosted personalities such as Wagner, Ruskin, Montale, Debussy, Balzac, and many others. It was featured in countless films and novels, and, simply put, it's part of the romantic imagery of the lagoon. Today it is synonymous with luxury and elegance, Venetian style.

398 **PALAZZO GRITTI**
Campo Santa Maria
del Giglio 2467
San Marco ①
+39 041 794 611
thegrittipalace.com

Located in a newly-renovated 16th-century palace, the Gritti Hotel offers one of the most beautiful views of the Canal Grande in the city. It has a restaurant with terrace, lounge, beauty spa, and even a cooking school.

399 **VENICE SIMPLON-ORIENT-EXPRESS**

DEPARTURE FROM:
Venezia Santa Lucia
railway station
Santa Croce ③
+44 (0)207 921 4000
belmond.com/experiences

Once in a blue moon, you may spot a train stopped at the platform in Venezia Santa Lucia railway station, that looks as if it has travelled through time from the early 1900s to the present day, with liveried staff. The spectacularly restored train is an homage to the past, when this train transported wealthy passengers from Paris to Istanbul. Today you can book a trip to several European capitals and spend the night in a luxurious suite, while sipping champagne and enjoying a delicious meal in a retro setting.

400 **BELMOND HOTEL CIPRIANI**

Fondamenta
San Giovanni 10
Giudecca ⑥
+39 041 240 801
belmond.com

Just picture one of those sultry days that you can only experience in Venice: what could be better than diving into the large swimming pool of this luxurious hotel and admiring the lagoon immersed in the quiet, while splashing in the cool water?

396 ISOLA SANTA CRISTINA

5 HOTELS WITH BEAUTY SPAS

(also) open to the public

401 **JW MARRIOTT VENICE RESORT & SPA**
Isola delle Rose ⑧
+39 041 852 1300
marriott.com

A magical place in the middle of the lagoon, shrouded in silence and tranquillity. This is what the Marriot hotel offers its guests with the beauty spa and wellness facilities. Also open to the public. You can check the website for prices and schedules.

402 **HILTON MOLINO STUCKY VENICE**
Fondamenta San Biagio 810
Giudecca ⑥
+39 041 272 3311
hilton.com

Even if you don't stay at the Hilton, this doesn't mean you cannot enjoy its spa. By purchasing the ticket, which – all things considered – is not that expensive, you'll have access to a sauna, a Turkish bath, a Jacuzzi and a relaxation area. Top off your day with an aperitif in the rooftop cocktail bar – a truly magical experience.

403 **HOTEL AI REALI DI VENEZIA**
Campo de la Fava 5527
Castello ⑤
+39 041 241 0253
hotelaireali.com

Hotel Ai Reali is located in a historic building just a few steps from Piazza San Marco. The spa is also open to external visitors and although not very large, it has swimming pools, a sauna, and a Turkish bath.

404 HOTEL NH COLLECTION VENEZIA MURANO VILLA

Fondamenta
Andrea Navagero 29
Murano ⑦
+39 041 273 1311
nh-hotels.com

The former Fornace De Majo, the go-to address glass factory which was famous for its chandeliers, recently reopened as the NH Collection Venezia Murano Villa. The hotel also has a spa, which will also open to the public once the pandemic winds down. In the meantime, you can already access the magnificent terrace that gives out onto the lagoon.

405 GRAND HOTEL DEI DOGI

Fondamenta
Madonna
dell'Orto 3500
Cannaregio ④
+39 041 220 8855
dahotels.com

The spa area of this elegant hotel is divided in two: a stone courtyard and an outdoor relaxation area located in a small garden, and an indoor, intimate and well-kept Turkish bath and swimming pool with a Jacuzzi.

50 WEEKEND ACTIVITIES

The 5 best BEACHES *near Venice*

406 **LIDO DI JESOLO**
Around Venice ⑩
jesolo.it

With its 18 kilometres of coastline, Jesolo will satisfy everyone: it's ideal for families and its nightlife attracts many young people every night. You can reach it from Venice with the boat to Punta Sabbioni. From there, a bus will take you directly to the beach.

407 **LIDO DI VENEZIA**
Lido di Venezia ⑧
veneto.eu

The Lido of Venice is the closest beach to the city. Among the various beach establishments, we recommend Bagni Alberoni, which is very comfortable and well equipped. Movie buffs will be happy to hear that the famous Venice Film Festival takes place on the Lido every September.

408 **ERACLEA MARE**
Around Venice ⑩
comune.eraclea.ve.it

Eraclea Mare offers expansive and well-serviced beaches. Some establishments, such as Mete Beach, are equipped for users with reduced mobility. They even have wheelchairs with special wheels for sand that can also go in the water.

409 **CAORLE**

Around Venice ⑩
caorle.eu

Caorle offers the ideal environment for children, with shallow water that gets deeper very gradually. If you're looking for an alternative to the beach, why not take a bike ride inland, to discover the *casoni* (traditional wooden and reed marsh houses) or a walk through the centre, or a visit to the cathedral and its round bell tower.

410 **CAVALLINO TREPORTI**

Around Venice ⑩
cavallino.info

A strip of land on the lagoon and the Adriatic Sea, the Cavallino area offers about 15 kilometres of beaches and pine forests. There are plenty of sport activities in nature to be enjoyed here. Check their website for the different itineraries on foot, by boat, and by bicycle.

5

HISTORICAL TOWNS

to visit near Venice

411 TREVISO
Around Venice ⑩
turismo.provincia.treviso.it

The Financial Times described this delightful town as a great destination to take a break from the hustle and bustle of Venice. Spend a day visiting the lively old town, full of cultural opportunities, its squares, its walls and its 12th-century cathedral. Then finish with a spritz in Piazza dei Signori, like a true local.

411 TREVISO

412 VICENZA

Around Venice ⑩
visitvicenza.org

If Palladio and its Basilica of the Redentore have made an impression on you, then you should visit Vicenza, where the famous architect built some equally grandiose masterpieces. Visit the Basilica Palladiana, the Olympic Theatre, the Palazzo of the Capitaniato and what has become the emblem of Palladian villas in the Veneto region, namely Villa Almerico Capra, known locally as 'La Rotonda'.

413 CHIOGGIA

Around Venice ⑩
infochioggia.com

Chioggia is also known as 'Little Venice', as it also has bridges and canals. The charm of its old centre and the wonders it contains are certainly worth a visit. Take water bus no. 11, which leaves from Piazza San Marco and continues via Pellestrina.

414 ASOLO

Around Venice ⑩
veneto.eu

Asolo is a small, timeless village in the hills of the Veneto. The actress Eleonora Duse preferred to live here, and the poet Carducci called it 'the City of 100 Horizons', probably because of the lovely mountain settings.

415 PADUA

Around Venice ⑩
turismopadova.it

Padua is the oldest university city in the Veneto region. It has many places of architectural and artistic interest, but if you had to choose one, you should definitely visit Giotto's Scrovegni Chapel, one of the greatest masterpieces of 14th-century painting. Booking is strongly recommended because it is so popular.

5
ANTIQUES MARKETS
on weekends

416 **MERCATINO ANTIQUARIATO CAMPO SAN MAURIZIO**
Campo San Maurizio
San Marco ①
+39 347 128 0848
mercatino camposanmaurizio.it

Explore one of the many flea markets, such as the one in San Maurizio, which is definitely worth a visit, to experience daily life in Venice. It is held in a delightful square of its own, boasts covered stalls, displaying antiques, Venetian crafts, and trinkets of all kinds. Sadly, it's only held five Sundays a year.

417 **MERCATINO DEI MIRACOLI**
Campo Santa Maria Nova
Castello ⑤
+39 041 271 0022

This delightful flea market takes place in the shade of the beautiful façade of the Church of Santa Maria Nova. You'll find a bit of everything here including books, collectibles, comic books. The market is held only ten days a year, which are chosen by the city government.

418 **MERCATINO 'BRIC À BRAC'**
Corso del Popolo
Mestre ⑩

Besides Venice, Mestre also has a nice flea market every first Saturday of the month. The event lasts all day, the market has about 45 stalls, which sell vintage clothes, extravagant antiques, and secondhand items.

419 MERCATINO DELLE ROBE DA MAR

Via Garibaldi
Castello ⑤
+39 041 271 0022

A great place for collectors and antiques lovers, this market is held every year around October. It takes place on the only proper street of Venice – Via Garibaldi – as opposed to in a *calle*, and is a good opportunity to visit one of the city's less touristy districts.

420 MERCATINO POLVERE DI RICORDI

Campo dell' Erberia and Campo San Silvestro
San Polo ③

Campo Sant'Agnese
Dorsoduro ②
+39 041 271 0022

This market takes place in different *campi*, depending on the day of the week. It has about 50 stalls, which are all managed by Venetians and where you can shop for anything from paintings to vinyl, prints and *murrine*, toys and silverware.

416 MERCATINO ANTIQUARIATO CAMPO SAN MAURIZIO

5 things to see in MURANO

421 CAM VETRI D'ARTE
Piazzale Colonna 1/B
Murano ⑦
+39 041 739 944
cam-murano.com

Like all timeless trades, the gestures of glassmaking transcend the boundaries of craftsmanship, turning it into a ritual. In this glassworks, you can watch masters as they create a vase or a small horse – the best way to fully appreciate all the expertise and effort that this art requires.

422 LA PERLA (AI BISATEI)
Campo S. Bernardo 7
Murano ⑦
+39 041 739 528

A rustic restaurant that is only open for lunch, that serves all the traditional delicacies, including lots of fish dishes. It is very popular with the locals, who are often given priority when waiting for a table, but this is also a badge of quality. They also serve *cicchetti* here, but only until noon, after which lunch is served!

423 MUSEO DEL VETRO
Fondamenta Marco Giustinian 8
Murano ⑦
+39 041 243 4914
museovetro.visitmuve.it

The museum, located in the Giustinian Palace, traces the history of glass from its origins, with iridescent pieces from the Roman era, and the works of the Most Serene Republic, up to the present day, with a selection of surprising and contemporary creations.

424 VENINI SPA

Fondamenta dei Vetrai 47
Murano ⑦
+39 041 273 7204
venini.com

When it comes to glass and Italian design, Venini is THE place to go. All the greatest national and international designers, architects, and artists have collaborated with this historic brand. Inside the museum you'll see, in addition to some iconic pieces, a significant number of sketches and drawings and some prototypes that were never taken into production.

425 THE GLASS CATHEDRAL, FORMER CHURCH OF SANTA CHIARA

Fondamenta Daniele Manin 1
Murano ⑦
+39 041 736 998
santachiaramurano.com

Since this 13th-century deconsecrated cathedral underwent a radical restoration, it has been transformed into an interesting place to tell the story of Murano's craftsmanship. Here you can see how glass is blown, as well as admire the sumptuous chandeliers and other colourful creations.

424 VENINI SPA

5

ACTIVITIES IN THE LAGOON

426 BOAT TRIP WITH THE FISHERMEN

STARTS AT: BURANO
Burano ⑨
+39 041 735 688
+39 339 273 9551
+39 388 325 5635 (ENG)
pescaburano.it

If you really want to understand the lagoon, its history and the ecosystem that characterises it, then trust Domenico and Enrico. These two fishermen have restored an old family *bragozzo* (local boat) and organise custom trips to corners of the lagoon that only the most experienced sailors can reach.

426 BOAT TRIP WITH THE FISHERMEN

427 **BOOK A CUSTOMISED GUIDED TOUR**

+39 388 325 5635
allisonzurfluh.ch

Allison loves the lagoon with all her heart and knows it like the back of her hand. Contact her for a journey that is meticulously tailored to your needs: she will point out the most authentic and unknown places of Venice as well as those most suitable for you.

428 **A CRUISE IN THE LAGOON ON A BRAGOZZO**

From Vignole
Around Venice ⑩
+39 349 743 1552
cruisingvenice.com

How does this sound for a plan: hop aboard a 1946 *bragozzo*, eat and drink amazing things prepared by the owner, a chef, while sailing quietly along the lagoon's canals? You'll visit some of the most famous islands, and wonderful hard-to-reach places like the Sant'Andrea fortress, while spending the day with a Venetian crew and international guests.

429 **BIKE RIDE ON THE LIDO**

Gran Viale S. Maria Elisabetta 79-A
Lido di Venezia ⑧
+39 041 526 1490
venicebikerental.com

As cycling in the historic centre is strictly forbidden, nothing stops you from taking a nice ride on the islands of the lagoon. The Lido lends itself particularly well to this activity, with its *murazzi* (walls built to protect the lagoon against storms) and the Alberoni beach. Take your own bicycle, or rent one directly on site.

430 **PASSEGGIATA PATRIMONIALE (THE HERITAGE WALK) IN MESTRE**

Mestre ⑩
+39 041 274 8503
live.comune.venezia.it

Mestre, where Venice's industry is located, is hardly ever taken into consideration when it comes to tourism, but there are many good reasons to take this walk. It's run by local scholars and guides, locals love it, and it's free. It usually takes place on the last weekend of September. Book in advance.

5 places to see in
BURANO

431 **BRUCO E PUPA ODD'S LAB**
Via Giudecca 41
Burano ⑨
+39 389 108 4770

This is not a place for cheap, mass-produced souvenirs. The owner of this delightful workshop-store creates colourful clay houses and precious silk scarves, treated with special processes. Everything here is simply unique.

432 **TRATTORIA AL GATTO NERO**
Via Giudecca 88
Burano ⑨
+39 041 730 120
gattonero.com

This extraordinary family-run *trattoria* serves typical dishes of Burano, such as *risotto di gò* (a tiny fish native to the lagoon) and homemade pasta with *granzeola* (European spider crab). The chef, Ruggero Bovo, is amazing. His son Massimiliano, a certified sommelier, manages the front of house and takes care of the wine list. A winning combo.

433 **EMILIA BURANO**
Piazza Baldassarre Galuppi 205
Burano ⑨
+39 041 735 245
emiliaburano.it

In this shop you'll find lace and textiles of unrivalled quality and a small museum that displays clothes and items so valuable that they are simply priceless. Learn more about the history of a family, of generations of women, who, for centuries, have been creating something that combines high craftsmanship with art.

434 **MUSEO DEL MERLETTO / LACE MUSEUM**

Piazza Baldassarre Galuppi 187
Burano ⑨
+39 041 730 034
museomerletto.visitmuve.it

In this small museum you can learn more about the history of lace, an exquisitely feminine art, from the 16th century onwards. You'll also learn how to recognise the various epochs of these delicate artefacts, according to different styles. The most fascinating room, however, is perhaps the last, where you might see the expert lace makers at work.

435 **CHURCH OF SAN MARTINO VESCOVO**

Piazza Baldassare Galuppi 20
Burano ⑨
+39 041 730 096

It's hard not to notice the bell tower of this exposed-brick church: not just because it's visible from all over the island, but mostly because it leans so heavily. Apparently the tower already started to crook during its construction. But don't be afraid: it has been stabilised and is constantly monitored.

435 CHURCH OF SAN MARTINO VESCOVO

5 other
ISLANDS
you should see

436 MAZZORBO
Isola di Mazzorbo ⑨

Mazzorbo is connected to the island of Burano by a single wooden bridge called Ponte Longo, from which you can enjoy a beautiful view of the lagoon. Recently, a once-lost grape known as Dorona is being grown again in the vineyards of Venissa, which produces a one-of-a-kind local speciality.

437 SAN FRANCESCO DEL DESERTO

San Francesco del Deserto ⑨

When you arrive on this small Franciscan oasis, you feel as if you are in a place that is suspended in time and space. Its name derives from a quotation attributed to Saint Francis, who praised its solitude. On weekends, you can even stay in the convent, surrounded by cypress trees.

438 LA CERTOSA

La Certosa ⑤

With its 22 hectares, La Certosa is one of the lagoon's largest islands. It is a remarkable natural refuge replete with thickets of ash and black and white poplars. It houses a modern nautical port that includes a dock, a sailing school and a shipyard.

439 SAN SERVOLO

San Servolo ⑧

The island of San Servolo feels rather sinister and it's easy to understand why the asylum for the insane used to be located here. Today it is home to the small but interesting 'Museum of Madness', which will make for an interesting stop if you're looking for something outside of the typical tourist itineraries.

440 SANT'ERASMO

Sant'Erasmo ⑨

Historically Sant'Erasmo is known as the vegetable garden of Venice. The island still follows the ancient rhythms of agriculture, and you will feel none of the frenzy in the city here. It's basically the perfect place for a walk in nature, and maybe a picnic on the little beach of the *Bacan*, where the locals traditionally like to come.

5 *amazing* NATURE RESERVES *near Venice*

441 **OASI LIPU CA' ROMAN**
Pellestrina
Around Venice ⑩
+39 340 619 2175
lipuvenezia.it

Thanks to its relative isolation, this small reserve is an exceptional habitat for all kinds of creatures. Its position in the lagoon, along one of the most important migration routes, makes it a perfect site for bird watching. Along the trails, you'll find educational panels. Between May and October, they organise boat trips to discover the local animal species.

442 **WWF'S OASIS OF VALLE AVERTO**
Via Pignara 4
Campagna Lupia
Around Venice ⑩
+39 041 518 5068
wwf.it

This large oasis has the typical landscape of the lagoon, with reeds and marshy areas, and forested areas where you can take a walk with an expert who can tell all there is to know about the local fauna and flora. The oasis is open to the public every first and third Sunday of the month.

443 **BOSCO DELL'OSELLINO**
Via Amerigo Vespucci
Mestre ⑩
+39 041 535 2224
boscoegrandiparchi.it

This small 8-hectare forest on the outskirts of Mestre, which was developed by the mayor, is now home to 13.000 plants and 35 different animal species. There is an observation tower and the raised wooden footpaths can be easily accessed with prams and wheelchairs.

444 **BOSCO DEL PARAURO**

Via Parauro, Mirano
Around Venice ⑩
+39 345 342 1353
napea.ve.it/bosco-del-parauro

This forest covers about 15 hectares. The trees are part of the local flora, and English oaks are predominant. A 1,3-kilometre trail winds its way through the woods. It is very accessible and perfect for a nice walk. There are also guided tours, workshops, and events, check the website for more information.

445 **WWF'S OASIS OF THE ALBERONI DUNES**

Piazzale Bagni Alberoni
Lido di Venezia ⑧
+39 348 268 6472
dunealberoni.it

The Oasis of the Alberoni is located at the southern tip of the Lido, and has a coastline that is populated by different species of birds, and dunes covered with dry grasslands. The undisputed stars of this reserve are the sea turtles and the Kentish plover, a small wading bird that lays its eggs directly on the beach.

443 BOSCO DELL'OSELLINO

5 strange places for some EXERCISE

446 **CA' SAN BOLDO**
Rio Terà San Tomà 2281
San Polo ③
+39 041 713 096
sanstin.com

It may seem incredible, but there is a red clay tennis court right in the centre of Venice. You can book it in advance and, if the members are not using it, you can play a game of tennis in Venice itself for the modest fee of 15 euro an hour.

447 **CIRCOLO GOLF VENEZIA**
Strada Vecchia 1
Lido di Venezia ⑧
+39 041 731 333
circologolfvenezia.it

A historic golf course, spanning 100 hectares, with 18 holes. Founded in 1928, it's the oldest in the region. Many champions from the past have walked this course, and several celebrities have frequented its bar.

448 **NORDIC WALKING VENEZIA SERENISSIMA**
Venice and islands
+39 347 497 2383
nordicwalking veneziaserenissima.it

If you don't have a boat, Nordic walking could be the perfect sport to keep active and enjoy the beauty of Venice. This association is very active and organises training in various parts of the city and also several trips in the lagoon. Check their website for more detailed information.

449 VENEZIA CERTOSA MARINA

La Certosa ⑤
+39 041 520 8588
vdvsport.it

In the new dock built on the island of La Certosa, the Vento di Venezia association offers sailing lessons for adults and children, as well as small cruises and sailing adventures. The island also has a wide range of additional services such as bicycle and kayak rental, restaurants and a hotel.

450 BOCCE BALL COURT OF SAN SEBASTIANO

Dorsoduro 2364
Dorsoduro ②
+39 041 275 0315
campobocce.it

It's difficult to find the green front door, and it's almost impossible to imagine that, behind it, there's a historic bocce ball court, with three courts that are available to members of the association. Walk-in players are welcome, and can enjoy the relaxed and timeless atmosphere of authentic Venice and, possibly, a couple of *ombre*.

450 BOCCE BALL COURT OF SAN SEBASTIANO

5 places to visit in
TORCELLO

451 **PONTE DEL DIAVOLO / THE DEVIL'S BRIDGE**
Lungo la Strada dal Porticciolo / Piazza Principale di Torcello
Torcello ⑨

There is a legend associated with this pretty brick bridge that has all the elements of a good story, including two star-crossed lovers, a witch, lost souls, a black cat, and – of course – the devil. You're free to believe it or not, but do take a walk across this bridge anyway.

452 **OSTERIA AL PONTE DEL DIAVOLO**
Fondamenta dei Borgognoni 10/11
Torcello ⑨
+39 041 730 401
osteriaalpontedeldiavolo.com

A break in this restaurant is an excellent idea, especially on a hot summer's day, because you can sit in the large gardens, which are also perfect for children. The kitchen serves Mediterranean fare with plenty of fish supplied by the local fishermen, so everything here is extremely fresh.

453 CASA MUSEO ANDRICH

Fondamenta dei Borgognoni 4/L
Torcello ⑨
+39 347 239 1861
museoandrich.com

Lucio Andrich was a painter as well as the last mosaic master at the Academy of Fine Arts in Venice. Today, his home has become a museum, which is run by his nephew. A unique place of art and nature where you can also enjoy the silence and the landscape of the lagoon.

454 ATTILA'S THRONE

Fondamenta dei Borgognoni
Torcello ⑨

In the square of the basilica of Santa Maria Assunta there is a massive stone throne dating back to the 5th century BC. Even though Attila probably never made it as far as the lagoon, the throne was nevertheless a symbol of power. In fact the governor of the island would sit on it during council meetings.

455 CHURCH OF SANTA FOSCA

Fondamenta dei Borgognoni 24
Torcello ⑨

The Church of Santa Fosca, which probably dates from the 12th century, is a solemn circular building. It has a portico supported by columns topped with Byzantine-style capitals. It stands next to the basilica of Torcello. Time really seems to have stopped here.

ANTONIO RIOBA'S NOSE

45 RANDOM FACTS & URBAN DETAILS

5 things you should
NEVER SAY *to a Venetian*

456 **WHERE CAN I GET A BUS?**

Beware: the only area of Venice's historic centre where vehicles (and this includes bicycles) are allowed is Piazzale Roma. From there on, you must rely on the city's public transportation, i.e., the water buses and water taxis. When planning your arrival, bear in mind that, while the water buses run all night, the times are obviously less frequent the later at night.

457 **WHERE CAN I FIND A SHOPPING CENTRE?**

The very nature of this one-of-a-kind city is absolutely incompatible with the hectic activity and large scale of a shopping centre. The closest thing perhaps to a shopping centre is the Fondaco dei Tedeschi. In any case, there is no shortage of shops of every kind and of great quality in Venice.

458 **MAY I HAVE A CAPPUCCINO (AFTER LUNCH)?**

This may sound fussy, but Venetians – and Italians – would never drink a cappuccino after lunch. Consider alternatives such as macchiato, decaf, *corretto* (with grappa added), and *ristretto*.

459 **WHEN'S THE NEXT HIGH WATER?**

Acqua alta, as it's known here, depends on a combination of winds and tides, so it's impossible to predict exactly when this will occur. In any event, you can check the weather forecast and various apps to avoid being caught unprepared. When high water is imminent, special alarms are also activated to warn the population.

460 **WHERE CAN I EAT LASAGNA?**

The answer is: in Bologna. While there is no doubt that lasagna is delicious, it has nothing to do with the Venetian culinary tradition. If a restaurant lists it on its menu, along with pizza or a cutlet, then you can be certain that it does not serve local cuisine.

5 *tricks for*
GETTING AROUND

461 VENEZIA UNICA CITY PASS

veneziaunica.it

On the Venezia Unica website you can buy different passes for public transportation and to access museums. When it comes to transportation, this solution is recommended even if you plan to stay in the city for just a few days: buying single tickets for the water buses will break the bank.

462 A GONDOLA RIDE FOR JUST 70 CENTS

Do you want to feel the thrill of being in a gondola but don't wish to spend a fortune on a tour? The gondola ferry or *traghetto* takes you from one side of the Canal Grande to the other, from Riva del Carbon, Santa Sofia, San Samuele and others for the very acceptable price of 70 eurocent, if you have a Venezia Unica pass. Otherwise it will cost you 2 euro. Please bear in mind that this ferry service always gives priority to workers.

463 CONNECTIONS TO THE MAINLAND

There's more than one way to reach Mestre from Venice: the easiest is to use the local trains (*regionale*) that connect the two stations and run pretty frequently (every 15 minutes or so). Otherwise you can hop on one of the buses departing from Piazzale Roma, which stop in various places in Mestre.

464 WATER TAXI

+39 041 240 6746
motoscafivenezia.it

If you want to book a taxi to and from Marco Polo Venice airport, you can do it in advance. Use the website to get a 5% discount. The average fare for the journey from the airport to Santa Lucia train station is around 110 euro for up to five people.

465 RENTING A BOAT

There are numerous islands in the lagoon and most of them are little-known. Some destinations (see the abandoned places list as an example) can't be reached via water bus. So why not rent a boat, with or without a crew, and organise a trip to the lagoon's most unknown destinations?

5
GARAGES
where you can leave your car

466 **ASM AUTORIMESSA COMUNALE**
Piazzale Roma 496
Santa Croce ③
+39 041 272 2394
actv.avmspa.it

This parking garage is one of the largest in Piazzale Roma, but if you're visiting the city during the peak season, we recommend booking through the website. Daily rates are around 23 to 29 euro, depending on the vehicle. Parking is free for up to 12 hours for people with disabilities.

467 **VENEZIA TRONCHETTO PARKING**
Isola Nuova del Tronchetto 33/M
Santa Croce ③
+39 041 520 7555
veniceparking.it

Located at Tronchetto, this garage is in a convenient location because it's in the immediate vicinity of the people mover, which allows you to get to the Santa Croce district and to the vaporetto stop that leads directly to Piazza San Marco. Around 21 euro to park for the day.

468 **PARCHEGGIO SABA STAZIONE VENEZIA MESTRE**
Viale Stazione 10
Mestre ⑩
+39 041 938 021
sabait.it

If you want to spend the day in Venice, parking your car in Mestre is a good alternative, as prices are lower than in Venice (around 16 euro a day) and trains leave from Mestre station to Venice Santa Lucia every ten minutes and cost only a few euro.

469 **GARAGE EUROPA MESTRE**
Corso del Popolo 55
Mestre ⑩
+39 041 959 202
garageeuropamestre.com

As the parking garage is located in Mestre, the tariffs are certainly cheaper than those in the city. Plus, it offers additional services such as luggage storage and shuttles to and from the airports of Venice and Treviso.

470 **PARCHEGGIO S. ANDREA AVM**
Piazzale Roma
Santa Croce ③
+39 041 272 2384
avm.avmspa.it

What's great about this parking garage is that it's located right in Piazzale Roma. Which means that you can drop off the car, cross the Ponte della Costituzione, and start your day immediately. But watch out for the steep prices: 7 euro for just two hours.

5 *bizarre* TOPONYMS

471 SOTOPORTEGO DELLA SCRIMIA
San Polo ③

The Sotoportego della Scrimia is located in San Polo. Until 1661, this area was called Calle del Garotti. Its name later changed, owing to the presence of a fencing school, hence the word *scrimia,* or swordsmanship.

472 FONDAMENTA DELLA STUA
San Polo ③

Literally *Stua* (dialect for stove or heater), these places were the equivalent of modern beauty salons, places where you could enjoy Turkish baths and massages, where women would gather, and sometimes also have secret affairs.

473 RIO TERÀ DEI ASSASSINI
San Marco ①

In the district of San Marco, near Campo Sant'Angelo. The rather distressing name (Former Canal of Assassins) derives from the number of murders that took place here, especially at night. To curb the phenomenon, the Republic of Venice even ordered that the street be fitted with public lighting.

474 CALLE PARADISO

San Polo ③

It's not clear whether this street takes its name (Paradise Street) from a noble family or *casada* that lived nearby or from the particularly lavish decorations that were put up here on Good Friday. The wedding of a Foscari to a Mocenigo is referenced on the arch at the top of the street, dispelling the former option.

475 PONTE DELLE TETTE

San Polo ③

Yes, this bridge's name means exactly what you think it does: the bridge of the tits. The whole area of the so-called *carampane* used to be the city's red-light district. From this bridge, passers-by could see the women at the windows that faced the bridge who exposed their breasts to attract potential customers.

473 RIO TERÀ DEI ASSASSINI

5 works of LITERATURE on Venice

476 **DEATH IN VENICE**
By Thomas Mann

Thomas Mann's masterpiece is a great read if you want to experience the atmosphere of the lagoon. He wrote: "Arriving in Venice from the train station was like entering a palace through the servants' entrance." Something that anyone who arrives in Venice by sea – perhaps mooring in Piazza San Marco – will confirm.

477 **THE FLAME**
By Gabriele d'Annunzio

Read *The Flame* by Gabriele d'Annunzio to see Venice through his impassioned eyes. The theme of the Übermensch, which was so dear to Nietzsche and is reworked here by the author, is a beautiful evocation of the city's culture and beauty.

478 THE STONES OF VENICE

By John Ruskin

John Ruskin was a leading art critic, writer, and painter, who was hugely influential in the 19th century. This book attests to his profound love of Venice and its architecture. He helped inspire a new approach to the modern discipline of restoration.

479 VENICE IS A FISH

By Tiziano Scarpa

Tiziano Scarpa is an Italian writer and playwright. Born and raised in Venice, he dedicated an original story in nine chapters to his city. Each section is linked to a body part. The atmosphere he conjures has little to do with physical places and much more with human experiences.

480 IF VENICE DIES

By Salvatore Settis

Venice's ecosystem is fragile and in decline, due to depopulation and historic buildings being sold off to foreign entrepreneurs. In this lucid and inspiring essay, Salvatore Settis reflects on the changes in the city, which are linked to economic factors. A useful read for mindful visitors.

5 *intriguing* **ESOTERIC** *symbols*

481 **CHURCH OF LA MADDALENA**
Campiello Maddalena 2205
Cannaregio ④

There are many clues in this church that point to freemasonry. The most obvious is the eye in a triangle above the entrance. The pediment features a Latin inscription that roughly translates to 'Wisdom has been built', a decidedly secular idea for a Catholic church. Obsolete Christian references or Masonic symbols?

482 **CHURCH OF SANT'APONAL**
Calle Sbianchesini 1135
San Polo ③

According to some sources, the Church of Sant'Aponal would have been the seat of the Freemasons, in operation since 1515, thanks to the sculptor and architect Pietro Lombardo, who had bought a plot at the base of the bell tower. The activities of the confraternity continued here until 1686, the year in which Venice decreed them to be illegal.

483 PALAZZO PISANI

Campiello Pisani 2810
San Marco ①
+39 041 522 5604
conservatorio venezia.net

The restoration of Palazzo Pisani unearthed, in what was previously little more than a warehouse, a seven-room apartment, which was probably a meeting place of a Masonic lodge. Today the building houses the Benedetto Marcello Conservatory of Venice and the renovated rooms are home to the Music Museum.

484 SCUOLA GRANDE DI SAN ROCCO

Calle Fianco de la Scuola 311
San Polo ③
+39 041 523 4864
scuolagrande sanrocco.org

The small and mysterious symbol carved on a stone to the left of the entrance is a secret hidden in full sight. It's easy not to notice this engraving, and its interpretation is still uncertain. Some assume it simply refers to the game of Nine Men's Morris, others see in it an esoteric scheme of three concentric squares.

485 CA' LEZZE

Fondamenta Misericordia 3597
Cannaregio ④

The 14th-century Palazzo Lezze is just one example of the architect Baldassare Longhena's work. On the façade, near the balconies, there are some bas-reliefs that feature symbols related to alchemical metamorphosis. Among them, you'll see images of animals representing the various stages of matter, up to purification.

5 *useful*
APPS & WEBSITES

486 **CAMMINANDOA VENEZIA.COM**

A useful website that suggests a series of interactive routes. Just choose a starting point from the list, such as the train station, the Rialto Bridge, Punta della Dogana and many others. Then select the type of historical sites you wish to visit and off you go.

487 **TURISMOVENEZIA.IT**

The tourism portal of the province of Venice offers all the information you'll need about this region, including cultural initiatives and food and wine. The section dedicated to the itineraries of Venice includes one without obstacles, meaning it's accessible and suitable for everyone, including wheelchair users.

488 **COMUNE.VENEZIA.IT**

Check out the city of Venice's website to keep up to date with all cultural and sports initiatives, as well as useful information like changes in public transportation routes or strikes, tide levels, and chances of *aqua alta*.

489 GIARDINI-VENEZIA.IT

Venice has some sumptuous historic gardens. Many are hidden or not easily accessible. This is why the Wigwam Club Giardini Storici Venezia was founded, to promote and enhance this particular aspect of the city's heritage. See their website for updates on tours and other activities.

490 CHORUS VENEZIA.ORG

It's estimated that there are around 148 churches in Venice, and the value of the artworks they contain is absolutely incalculable. If you want to visit all of them, it's best to check the Chorus Venezia website, where you can buy multi-venue tickets and tours that will take you to the most valuable sites.

5 MARATHONS *for runners in Venice*

491 VENICE MARATHON
huaweivenice marathon.it

Venicemarathon organises a series of competitive and non-competitive sporting events, including a 42-kilometre marathon that starts from the Riviera del Brenta and leads to Venice. Then there's the 10-kilometre race, open to everyone, which covers the last section of the full itinerary.

492 5.30 VENEZIA

The 5.30 association organises non-competitive itineraries in various Italian cities to promote a healthy lifestyle. The run starts at 5.30 am on a work day and is 5,3 kilometres long. In Venice, the event generally takes place around July.

493 SU E ZO PER I PONTI / UP AND DOWN THE BRIDGES
suezo.it

Su e Zo is a non-competitive walk suitable for everyone. It's usually scheduled in April and has a very high attendance every year. Walkers follow two routes, of six and twelve kilometres, that wind through the streets and bridges of the city, and both end in Piazza San Marco.

494 QUASI NIGHT RUN

runningclub veneziaasd.it

The Running Club Venezia was founded by a group of friends who wanted to share their passion for running. Every year, they organise the 'Quasi night run', a non-competitive race that is held at sunset and which winds its way through some of Venice's most iconic sights.

495 VENICE NIGHT TRAIL

venicenighttrail.it

The Venice Night Trail is held in April, in the charming atmosphere of the historic centre, which, at night, looks and feels completely different. The route is a 16-km loop, starting and ending in San Basilio, and includes 51 bridges.

5
LUCKY CHARMS

496 **ANTONIO RIOBA'S NOSE**
Campo dei Mori
Cannaregio ④

On the corner of Palazzo Mastrelli you'll find three statues. Legend has it that they represent three brothers, who were fraudulent merchants, and who were turned to stone as punishment for their misdemeanours. Ever since the nose of one of the brothers was replaced with a steel protuberance, the people of Venice have taken to touching it, like a good luck charm.

497 **RED BRICK HEART**
AT: SOTOPORTEGO DEI PRETI
Salizada del Pignater
Castello ⑤

The red brick heart inside the arch of Sotoportego dei Preti recalls the love of the fisherman Orion for the serene Melusine. Legend has it that, if lovers touch it, one of their wishes may come true.

498 HANDLES OF THE SAN CANZIAN BRIDGE

Sotoportego del Traghetto
Castello ④⑤

Immediately after the San Canzian bridge you'll find the Sotoportego del Traghetto, which bears engravings from the Risorgimento period (which ends with the Italian unification, 1815-1870). There you'll find the 'handles' also known as the double anchors. They say that touching them brings good luck, prosperity, and even fertility.

499 TWO COLUMNS IN PIAZZA SAN MARCO

Piazza San Marco
San Marco ①

The two columns in pink marble and granite mark the end of one of the most beautiful squares in the world. Yet, local folklore has it that walking through them will bring bad luck. That is because public executions were once held here... Best to avoid it!

500 CHURCH OF SAN MOISÈ

Campo San Moisè 1390/A
San Marco ①

In the Church of San Moisè you'll find the remains of John Law, the inventor of the banknote. Apparently, rubbing the doormat at the entrance will help you turn your financial fortune for the better.

INDEX

COLOPHON

EDITING *and* COMPOSING – Anna Sardi

TRANSLATION – Luisa Grigoletto and Sandy Logan

GRAPHIC DESIGN – Joke Gossé and doublebill.design

PHOTOGRAPHY – Corrado Piccoli – corradopiccoli.com

COVER IMAGE – San Trovaso shipyard (secret 241)

The addresses in this book have been selected after thorough independent research by the author, in collaboration with Luster Publishing. The selection is solely based on personal evaluation of the business by the author. Nothing in this book was published in exchange for payment or benefits of any kind.

D/2022/12.005/12
ISBN 978 94 6058 3209
NUR 512, 510

Second edition, May 2022 – First reprint, May 2022
lusterpublishing.com – THE500HIDDENSECRETS.COM
info@lusterpublishing.com

Printed in Italy by Printer Trento.

MIX
Paper | Supporting responsible forestry
FSC® C015829